ML

12/93

EZRA POUND:
The Voice of Silence

by
Alan Levy

THE PERMANENT PRESS
Sag Harbor, New York 11963

A PREFACE TO THE FIRST THREE
PORTRAIT BOOKS

When my profiles-in-depth of W. H. Auden, Vladimir Nabokov, and Ezra Pound first appeared in the New York *Times Magazine* in the early 1970's, I received many letters and a few transatlantic calls from editors and publishers who all voiced the same regret: that these articles must die the natural deaths of yesterday's paper or last week's Sunday supplement.

Their solutions, no matter how winningly phrased did not grab me – for I had heard their gists and piths before. Basically, these proposals boiled down to two. The Vertical Approach: "Why don't you paste them up, together with some others you've done, and we'll publish a collection?" To which my response was: "For whom?". . . The Horizontal Approach: "How about expanding this one [or that one] into a definitive biography?" The answer came particularly easily in Pound's case: "It took me two weeks to get two hundred words of quotes from him, so I don't think I'll live long enough to do a full-length biography." At the time, Pound was eighty-six and I was thirty-nine.

I also recognized that, from each of the three writers, I had drawn all or almost all that personal contact was going to elicit. And yet I wasn't ready to let go of them.

The solution dawned when one editor, Howard Greenfeld, began by reminding me: "These are all old men. For one or more of them, this may be the last public appearance before the obituary notices." Howard went on to stress my obligation to students and others who were just starting to discover and read these authors: to put my work, their output, and their lives into some solid, useful order. I realized that, when I had been an undergraduate at Brown University and a graduate student at Columbia, and just starting to read Pound and Auden (Nabokov was still "too new" then), I certainly would have welcomed an informed introduction to them as living men rather than assigned authors.

Howard Greenfeld being an American editor living in Europe in the next country to mine, he and I were able to continue the discussion over many months – and out of it has come this small cottage industry of PORTRAIT BOOKS: published for library, critical, gift-giving, student, and general use. These first three are – and the Portrait Books to come in future years will be – works of enthusiastic journalistic scholarship researched and written, firsthand, by one man who knew his subjects well and intensely. . .who read everything by them that he could lay hands on before and after he profiled them. . .and who likes and cares for what he is writing about. These books have a uniform format – though the lengths and styles of the components can be as different as Pound is from Auden is from Nabokov.

Part 1: THE MAN. A biographical portrait, drawn from my initial magazine interviews. They are never padded, though sometimes they are fleshed out with material that was omitted or lost to the magazine's editorial, puritanical, or space needs. Nor are the magazine profiles drastically reworked, except to fit the needs of each book and bring it up-to-date. All of the first three heroes have died in the interim between article and book, but each first chapter remains a meeting with the living man in the context of his living word.

Part 2: QUOTES. A mosaic of words by and about the man you've just met. This section is organized with an ear to the rhythm as well as the flavor of whatever he has done to merit your attention.

Part 3: An essay on EXPERIENCING him, not just reading him or reading about him. Written conversationally, this is a verbal map, with a few guidelines, for a voyage of discovery in which you share some of What It's Like and How It Feels to be reading Pound or Nabokov or Auden, hearing him on records, and perhaps attending his plays or movies. It is narrated with my own personal insights and affection for the works. I must emphasize that this is NOT a critical essay. At my most waspish, I may warn you off a redundant lesser work or vent my outrage at the kind of critical study that erects barriers of boredom and trivia between you and the artist – so I never want to feel guilty of the same crime against literature. And this chapter should be read NOT as a substitute for actually experiencing the artist, but as an appetizer or as a companion to the essential experience.

Part 4: A comprehensive BIBLIOGRAPHY that does what most bibliographies I've seen don't do: it takes cognizance of paperback and hardcover reissues, instead of merely listing all the relevant details of the original 1910 or 1967 edition, now out of print, by a publisher who is now out of business. And it contains Library of Congress catalog listings as well as Dewey decimal shelf numbers. This will tell you where to look in your own library's alpahbetical card file and may even enable you to go directly to the specific shelf where you'll find a certain book or related works. In this effort, I was blessed in the 1970s by the heroic labors of Joseph H. Podoski of Washington, D.C., a retired Librarian of Congress and in the 1980s with the assistance of my daughter Monica and my wife Valerie on visits to the Library of Congress.

Part 5: A simple factual CHRONOLOGY of the man's life and career for compact easy reference. For this common-sense suggestion, I am grateful to Prof. Alden Todd (author of *Finding Facts Fast*), who had the common sense to suggest it.

These books are illustrated with photos by the man I consider the best portrait photographer working in Europe today: Horst Tappe of Montreux, Switzerland. A photographer of rare cultural and personal sensitivity as well as talent, Horst has often been the key who opened the doors to my audiences with great men.

Ezra Pound died in 1972, W. H. Auden in 1973, and Vladimir Nabokov in 1977. All three of them long ago earned their immortality, but it is my hope that these small books of mine will ease the path for your understanding and enjoyment of WHY they will live on.

PORTRAIT BOOKS: The First Trilogy
1. EZRA POUND: The Voice of Silence
2. W. H. AUDEN: In the Autumn of the Age of Anxiety
3. VLADIMIR NABOKOV: The Velvet Butterfly

Dedication:
To
EZRA POUND
and
OLGA RUDGE
who put me
"in touch with reality"

CONTENTS

THE MAN: "EZRA POUND IS NO PANCAKE"

Take thought:
I have weathered the storm,
I have beaten out my exile.

— "The Rest" (1913)

Toward the end of his life, Ezra Pound, eighty-six when I met him and eighty-seven when he died in Venice, found yet another eloquent new voice: silence. This American bard whose *Cantos* transformed the language of English poetry. . .this early champion and benefactor of James Joyce, Robert Frost, Ernest Hemingway, D. H. Lawrence and T. S. Eliot. . .this inspired midwife to Eliot's *Waste Land*. . .spoke mostly in monosyllables — when he spoke at all.

Some say this had to do with the fatigue of age plus a physical collapse that followed his thirteen years of incarceration as a political prisoner of his own United States: 1945 to 1958, including three weeks in an outdoor cage that the U.S. Army built to hold him in solitary confinement near Pisa; a fortnight in a District of Columbia Jail while awaiting trial for nineteen counts of treason based on his wartime broadcasts for the fascist radio in Rome; and more than a dozen years in Washington's St. Elizabeth Hospital for the Criminally Insane. Some say Pound's silence spelled his disgust with life and mankind. Some say Pound had discovered that words have more to do with lies and misunderstanding than with communication. Once, a stranger asked him: "Where are you living now?"

"In hell," Pound replied.

"Which hell?"

"Here, here," the poet said, pressing both hands to his heart.

The English poet Peter Russell (long resident in Venice) attributed some of Pound's silence to "the histrionic side of Ezra. He can say *yes* and *no* with so many shades of inflection that it becomes a language in itself. The rest, I think, is that he's entered a period of meditation and contemplation. For Ezra, after all, it's all been said. He's heard everything most people have to say. He's said everything he has to say — and he's said it magnificently."

In 1963, early in his silence, Ezra Pound seemed to have confirmed this in a rare outburst of explanation to Italian journalist Grazia Livi. *"I have lived all my life believing that I knew something,"* Pound told her. *"But then a strange day came and I realized I knew nothing. And thus words became devoid of meaning. I know nothing now. I have arrived too late at the greatest uncertainty."*

A tall, blonde Austrian painter, Liselotte Höhs, referred to Pound's silence as "his language of listening." Whatever one called it, though, it had been going on for more than a decade when I came to Venice in late 1971. In the early 1960's, however, when Liselotte first met Pound soon after she had settled in Venice, she was "one of the few people he spoke to – and he went on speaking to me long after he stopped speaking to his oldest friends. We made animated chit-chat – about the weather, about *acqua alta* [high water that threatens to engulf Venice every autumn], about people we know. Nothing serious; I'm a girl with no philosophy. I had never read any of his poetry, but now I wanted to. So I started out by reading his poems about the part of Venice where we both live. And when I told him this, he stopped speaking to me. We're still friends – he likes to come and sit in my studio or my garden – but I think he's afraid I've become an intellectual."

Forewarned that there would be difficulties, I journeyed to Venice on one of autumn's last sunny afternoons – and then waited ten days while my first meeting with Pound was scheduled, canceled, and rescheduled by his devoted mistress and companion, the retired violinist Olga Rudge. But when I was at last invited over, my welcome was wholehearted – for there were few half-measures or compromises in the life Ezra Pound led. Thus, I ended my stay in Venice with four consecutive days in Pound's presence, including two lunches together and a trip out to the Rialto by gondola and on foot – time enough to ascertain that, even with a minimum of spoken words, this most enduring of twentieth-century poets retained his *persona* of a rapscallious old polecat:

> *Winter is icumen in,*
> *Lhude sing Goddamm,*
> *Raineth drop and staineth slop,*
> *And how the wind doth ramm!*
> > *Sing: Goddamm.*
> *Skiddeth bus and sloppeth us,*
> *An ague hath my ham.*

Freezeth river, turneth liver,
        Damn you, sing: Goddamm.
Goddamm, Goddamm, 'tis why I am, God-
damm,
        So 'gainst the winter's balm.
Sing goddamm, damm, sing Goddamm,
Sing goddamm, sing goddamm,
DAMM.

My troubles gaining entry to the narrow three-room triplex house that Olga Rudge has owned since 1928 – and where she and Pound lived most of each year – were the aftermath of shattering distrust engendered by the previous summer's publication of a memoir called *Discretions.* (Pound's own 1923 "autobiographical reverie" was called *Indiscretions.*) The author of *Discretions* was their forty-six-year-old illegitimate daughter, now Princess Mary de Rachewiltz. The child they had wanted and whom Olga Rudge, at least, had long envisioned as Pound's ultimate biographer, portrayed her father as a kindly, if distant, *"Babbo"* and her mother as a selfish shoe-swiping *"Mamile."* Thus, yet another Greek tragedy was being enacted in the long life of Ezra Pound – who (back in 1965, after several years of silence) turned to a friend and spoke, out of the blue, in a Learlike moan: *"I have never made a person happy in my life."*

(There was also a *Mrs.* Ezra Pound, the former Dorothy Shakespear, known even in his lifetime as "Pound's official widow." One of his early poems, "Canzoni – To Be Sung Beneath a Window," was written for her. Upon his 1958 discharge from the insane asylum, he was given into her custody and – while he soon rejoined Olga Rudge – Dorothy Shakespear Pound functioned in nearby Merano as a Committee for Ezra Pound. In 1971, she published a book, *Etruscan Gate: A Notebook,* containing her own drawings and watercolors. She outlived her husband by thirteen months, and died at eighty-seven on December 8, 1973. There is also a legitimate son, Omar Shakespear Pound – fourteen months younger than Princess Mary. An American GI toward the end of World War II, Omar Pound was later a teacher at Roxbury Latin School in Boston and professor of Islamic history at Cambridge University in England.)

Not long after complications started threatening my visit, the Swiss intermediary who had arranged it flew to Venice to plead on my behalf. A trusted friend of Pound's and Olga Rudge's for more than a decade, he was kept waiting nearly seventy-two hours before being called at noon and invited over for 2:30 P.M. I waited in my hotel room, staring out at a swollen Grand Canal and trying to read newsmagazines, until the phone rang at 7:30 P.M. "Get right over here," said the Swiss, "before anyone's mind changes."

("I almost had you here at four o'clock," the Swiss told me later. But then the phone rang twice – friends telling them the *acqua alta* was coming. Venice shuts off all electricity and central heating when that happens and so Olga Rudge had to run out to buy kindling wood. She even borrowed some rubber boots for me. It was all quite frantic for an hour or two before I could work the conversation back to you.")

Dashing out of my hotel, I caught *vaporetto* number 1 – a large public motorboat that crisscrosses the Grand Canal – for the two-minute, five-cent ride from San Marco to the Church of Santa Maria della Salute. Then I hurried through streets that were glistening and wet (though it hadn't rained all day), and, in five minutes, I was ringing the lion-faced doorbell of Olga Rudge's home.

A British-accented, very Bostonian native of Youngstown, Ohio, Olga Rudge struck me, in her seventies, as tough, starchy, and beautifully wrinkled. She was dressed to go out, but ushered me in warmly. "Watch out for *that*," she cautioned, pointing to a thin, foot-high slab of brownish-white marble rising up from the threshold like bread from a toaster. "Sooner or later, somebody will break his neck on it," she explained, "but I had it put there to keep out the *acqua alta*. The workmen who installed it tapped their heads. They insist that the water doesn't come in from the street, but seeps up from below and this will keep it in. Well, we will see who is right."

Taking off her coat and hanging up mine, she asked me point-blank: "Are you a sensitive plant? . . . Because Mr. Pound has a temper – and while that's good for him, it isn't always good for others who aren't prepared for it. He's in bed now."

She led me up a flight of wooden stairs, and as she did, she said: "Do you know Mr. Eliot's poem that begins 'My name is Tough'? . . . Well, be tough."

Thus fortified, I was presented to the thin, bony man in blue pajamas who was sitting up in bed – a sofa bed that had been opened full length and littered with colored pillows. The famous red beard

4

was white and wispier now; the haunting blue eyes clouded, though Pound had undergone successful cataract surgery. He was cracking his knuckles and his hands were so tightly clasped that he seemed to be scraping bone. But he unclasped long enough for me to take his right hand and shake it.

"Mr. Levy moves fast," my hostess told him. "I was all ready to go down to the *imbarcadero* to fetch him when he rang the bell."

And Ezra Pound spoke to me: *"You were supposed to be here at teatime."*

The voice was nasal, a little higher-pitched than the various Caedmon and Spoken Arts recordings I'd heard, but absolutely firm. No explanation of the *acqua alta* delay was given. "I'll leave you two alone," was all Olga Rudge said before continuing upstairs, where the Swiss intermediary was waiting. I took the chair beside the bed and began my questions – telling Pound briefly how I came to his poetry in college, through Oscar Williams' *Little Treasury of Modern Poetry* with its

> *Sing for love and idleness,*
> *Naught else is worth the having.*
>
> *Though I have been in many a land,*
> *There is naught else in living.*
>
> *And I would rather have my sweet,*
> *Though rose-leaves die of grieving,*
>
> *Than do high deeds in Hungary*
> *To pass all men's believing.*
> *– "An Immorality" (1912)*

I recited the poem from memory and I quoted from the next generation of poets: W. H. Auden's assertion that "there are few living poets. . .who could say 'My work would be the same if Mr. Pound had never lived.' Then I quoted from yet another generation of poets: Harvey Shapiro, who told me: "Ezra Pound remains very much alive in the States as a strong, maybe the strongest, influence on young poets today." And I asked Pound: "Have you any reaction to this?"

Silence.

"How closely do you follow the American literary scene today?"

Silence

5

"Are there any younger writers you particularly admire or detest?"

Silence again, but the eyes flashed, so I waited. And then it came like an angry thunderclap: *"Disorder! Disorder! I can't be blamed for all this damned disorder."*

(The late Pier Paolo Pasolini, the leftist Roman film director, at his second meeting with Pound, quoted from Canto LXXVI – *"woe to them that conquer with armies/and whose only right is their power"* – and remarked to Pound: "These are pacifist verses. Would you like to participate in one of the demonstrations which are taking place in America to help the world remain at peace?" Pasolini provoked this reply from Pound: *"I think the intentions are good, but I do not think these demonstrations are the right answer. I see things from another angle. As I wrote in a draft for a recent Canto: 'When one's friends hate one another/ how can there be peace in the world?'"* To a Sicilian poet seeking long-range advice, Pound replied: *"Curiosity – advice to the young – curiosity."*)

A Venetian publisher had issued an expensive volume of photos called *Spots and Dots: Ezra Pound in Italy,* purporting (in the words of the photographer, Vittorugo Contino) "to show Pound the man, now at the end of his life, without thoughts of his past." I told Pound I considered this cruel.

"Waaa-ll," he said, *"I think it lacks coherence."*

To a suggestion – posed in that same book – that literature may spring from hate, Pound responded: *"Part of literature seems to spring from hate, but its vitality is not in the hatred."*

I posed further questions and elicited naught else until I asked whether the economic theories that led him to embrace Mussolini (and broadcast for him in wartime) have perhaps been absolved or justified by recent monetary history. Then Pound's eyes flashed like blinking signals and his classic Grecian head came up off the pillows with these words: *"I told* [the Swiss] *this was not to be one of those interviews."*

"I didn't know that, sir, I said. "We'll keep it a conversation of sorts." The head reclined, but the eyes glinted warily. I asked about the photographer who was due to start work the next day.

"I think there have been altogether too many photographs."

Deeming it unwise to push either issue or simply babble at Ezra Pound, I sat in silence and watched the glint of temper fade from his face. Then, still saying nothing, I watched him crack and scrape and unscrape his knuckles. Then, in the prolonged mutual silence, he whistled! It was just one toot, but I laughed, he winked, and everything was going to be all right! The silence resumed.

Hearing the silence, Olga Rudge came halfway down the stairs and, leaning over a loose banister, asked if I would "like to listen to His Master's Voice?" Pound nodded and I went upstairs to his studio, where he still sat at a desk every day and where Olga Rudge and the Swiss had been waiting.

Olga Rudge played a record of excerpts from a Spoleto Festival in the mid-sixties, which included Pound reading Canto XVI: the snarling, cursing, many-tongued, many-accented "War Canto" that swirls from the Franco-Prussian War through the First World War (*"And Bimmy was 19 when he went to it/And his major went mad in the control pit"*) and into Bolshevik Russia (*"Ain't yeh heard? Say, ve got a rheffolution.'/ That's the trick with a crowd,/ Get 'em into the street and get 'em moving"*). Written in the early 1920's and today almost too contemporary to bear, Canto XVI exemplifies the *Cantos* (120 in all) as Pound's own history of the world and the most autobiographical long poem in the English language. It was modeled after Dante. But, just as Shakespeare peopled his Denmark and Italy with eloquent Englishmen, so did Pound people Confucian China and Homeric Greece with blunt-spoken Americans (*"And Kung said/ 'You old fool, come out of it,/ Get up and do something useful' "*). And, whatever the *Cantos'* claim to immortality, Pound's epic poem more than justifies Charles Norman's assertion that "the *Cantos* is to poetry, or the development of poetry, what Joyce's *Ulysses* was to the novel. . . . Its range being wide, and its technique novel, its influence has been enormous. From *The Waste Land* on, no poem of any length has escaped the influence of the structure and flow of Pound's *Cantos.*"

Or, as Ernest Hemingway wrote:

Any poet born in this century or in the last ten years of the preceding century who can honestly say he has not been influenced by or learned greatly from the work of Ezra Pound deserves to be pitied rather than rebuked. It is as if a prose writer born in that time should not have learned from or been influenced by James Joyce or that a traveler should pass through a great blizzard and not have felt its cold or a sandstorm and not have felt the sand and the wind. The best of Pound's writing – and it is in the *Cantos* – will last as long as there is any literature.

On the top floor of Olga Rudge's,she and I and the Swiss perched on an opened sofa bed and listened to "His Master's voice." Olga Rudge looked as well as listened – watching the record with the rapture of a young girl or a Back Bay dowager at the Friday afternoon Boston Symphony. And I remarked, as many have done before, on the poet's possession of a playwright's ear. I asked my hostess if Pound had ever written a play.

"I don't really know," she replied. "There was, of course, *Women of Trachis.*" (Pound's translation of Sophocles, completed in St. Elizabeth's, was performed on the BBC Third Programme in 1954 and then on stage in Berlin and Darmstadt.) Later, on our way downstairs, we tiptoed in case the poet was sleeping – but he was watching us, so Olga Rudge asked: "Well, Pound, did you ever write an original play? There are rumors, you know."

He pursed his lips and said: *"Neauouw."*

She said: "What do you mean, *neauouw?* That's not the same as *no.*"

For a moment, he was more sheepish than catlike as he said: *"Waaall, I started one and tore it up."*

Olga Rudge asked: "And is it going to turn up all in one piece like *Patria Mia?*" (A "lost essay" on American civilization that he wrote in 1910 and 1911. Mislaid by an English publisher in 1915, it was discovered and issued in 1950.)

No answer from Pound, but the eyes danced merrily.

We bade Pound good night. Downstairs, the Swiss and I drank gin-and-tonic with Olga Rudge. There was no mention that evening of Her Daughter's Book. Nor was it visible on any of the many bookshelves that did include virtually every book written by or about Pound, Joyce and Eliot, as well as a dozen works of Samuel Beckett in British paperback; Walt Whitman, Mary Renault, Leslie Fiedler, and Norman Mailer's volume of poetry, *Death for the Ladies, and Other Disasters.*

Olga Rudge explained why she had to be so protective of Pound:

"We get hippies, coming here and when we're in Rapallo. They have embraced the wisdom of Ezra Pound, but they haven't read him. One of them pitched a tent outside; I gave him coffee, but no Ezra. Another was so persistent in his devotion that I told him, 'I'll let you in if you can quote one line of Ezra Pound – any line of the thousands he's written.' He couldn't.

"Others come to read him *their* poetry. They don't know *his* poetry, but they want him to praise theirs. And *their* craftsmanship is so poor. There is no oral tradition anymore. It's all publicity.

"Then we get the promoters. Fat young men with silk shirts and bleached sideburns who show up with two air tickets to London and leaflets announcing that they're sponsoring a poetry reading by Ezra Pound in the Albert Hall. I send them and their tickets and their handbills away, too.

"Then there are the journalists. They insist on what they call 'the public's right to know' and they ask me 'Who do you think you are, anyway?' When I woke up early one morning at our place in Sant'Ambrogio [near Rapallo] and found one of them had been sleeping all night in a deck chair on our terrace – and was still there! – I flushed him out with a garden hose."

Among the nuisances must be numbered Allen Ginsberg, who descended on Pound (according to Olga Rudge) "like a big lovable dog who gives you a great slovenly kiss and gets lots of hair all over you." Ginsberg arrived in Rapallo with an entourage one summer in the late 1960's. They made their presence known by performing Hare Krishna outside Pound's door. Amused and aware of his fellow poet's stature, Pound had Ginsberg & Co. invited in for coffee. Olga Rudge's first question, "Would you like to wash your hands?," caused her guests to exchange looks of horror, although it was not meant as the euphemistic bourgeois gentility they took it for. "Their hands were dirty and I thought they would want to wash them," she told me.

Ginsberg's first question to Pound was even more bourgeois: "Do you people need any money?"

Olga Rudge laughed and said: "No. At our age, what we need is time." And Pound added that he was content with the *"million-dollar view"* from their terrace.

A little later, Ginsberg & Co. were again horrified – this time to learn that Ezra Pound had never heard of Bob Dylan. "He covered that gap in Ezra's education," Olga Rudge reported, "by sending him several Dylan records, which Ezra didn't enjoy at all."

Still later, Olga Rudge was appalled to read an interview in which Ginsberg chided Pound for his bourgeois background and values – and told of his own good deeds, including buying Pound $75 or $85 worth of Dylan records. "It was all about money, not about time or poetry," Olga Rudge observed.

And, much, much later, she was disgusted while attending a

Poetry International symposium in London at which Richard Eberhart glibly defined Pound as a "pro-war" and "anti-Semitic" poet – whereupon Allen Ginsberg chimed in gratuitously: "And anti-Negro."

To Olga Rudge, though, the worst tormentors "are the so-called 'biographers.' Some of them actually publish 'biographies' and one of them, who spent a total of fifteen minutes in our presence before I got rid of him, had the audacity to 'acknowledge' my patience and persistent help over a period of years. They ring my bell and announce they are writing books that "will tell both sides.' *Both* sides? Both sides! What do they think we are? Ezra Pound is no pancake!"

> *The age demanded an image*
> *Of its accelerated grimace,*
> *Something for the modern stage,*
> *Not, at any rate, an Attic grace;*
>
> *Not, not certainly, the obscure reveries*
> *Of the inward gaze;*
> *Better mendacities*
> *Than the classics in paraphrase!*
> — from *Hugh Selwyn Mauberley*
> *(1919-1920)*

Ezra Loomis Pound, author of *Jefferson and/or Mussolini* and "The Jew, Disease Incarnate,*" was no more of a pancake than the earth is flat. But the mental baggage that strangers bring to his name succeeds all too often in crushing the juices of life and vitality, excellence and experiment that course through his career. At any point in his lifetime, it could be (and has been) said that "Ezra Pound was *somewhere to be found.*" It has also been said of Pound: "A man may be so far left he seems right, and so far right he seems wrong."

He was born October 30, 1885, in Hailey, Idaho (a few miles from Ketchum, where his friend Hemingway ended his life in 1961), but he grew up in Philadelphia after his father, Homer, was named assistant assayer of the United States Mint. Just as the very name Pound has monetary significance, this boyhood background had some bearing on the economic theories that did him in.

At the Mint, the boy saw – and remembered – people bringing in "gold-bricks" peddled by swindlers, that proved to be gilded

---

*Published only in Italian (1939) by the newspaper *Meridiana di Roma* as "l' ebreco malattia incarnata."

lead . . . workmen telling visitors who inquired about free samples that "you're welcome to keep this bag of gold if you can carry it away," which proved impossible . . . and, after the 1892 Presidential election, *"silver I saw, as no Aladdin, for when [Grover] Cleveland was elected, there was the recount of four-million in the Mint vaults, the bags had rotted, and the men half-naked with open gas flares, shoveled it into the counting machines, with a gleam on tarnished discs."* By the time he was seven, he also knew –from his parents' struggles to keep up with their genteel neighbors on a civil servant's salary – that his playmates were richer than he was.

A couple of years younger than (and much disliked by) his classmates, this bright, sensitive, yet extroverted lad

> *knew at 15 pretty much what I wanted to do. I resolved that at 30 I would know more about poetry than any man living, that I would know what was accounted poetry everywhere, what part of poetry was "indestructible," what part could not be lost by translation and – scarcely less important – what effects were obtainable in one language only and were utterly incapable of being translated.*
>
> *In this search I learned more or less of nine foreign languages. I read Oriental stuff . . . I fought every University regulation and every professor who tried to make me learn anything except this, or who bothered me with "requirements for degrees."*

Emerging with a Ph.B. degree in 1905 from Hamilton College and an M.A. in 1906 from the University of Pennsylvania, Pound was already embittered, if not embarrassed, by the financial fate that awaited the educated graduate, particularly the poet, so he wrote this lament:

> *Go little verse,*
> *Go forth and be damned*
> *Throughout your limited sphere*
> *But prithee tell*
> *The bards in hell*
> *Who live on nothing a year*
> *That a Master of Arts*

And a man of parts
Is doing the same thing here.

When his first and last teaching post, as instructor of Romance languages at Wabash College, ended in dismissal after a stranded burlesque chorus girl was found sleeping in his bed (Pound claimed he slept on the floor and was not only fully clothed, but wrapped chastely in his topcoat) he sailed in 1908 for Venice – "an excellent place to come to from Crawfordsville, Indiana." This stay in Venice lasted only a few months – long enough to publish, at his own expense, his first collection of poems, *A Lume Spento;* to audition (unsuccessfully) to be a gondolier; and to regard the Venetian sun as a fixed point of return and repose that persisted throughout his life:

> *Thou that hast given me back*
> *Strength for the journey.*
> *Thou that hast given me*
> *Heart for the tourney.*
> – "Alma Sol Veneziae"

For a rookie American poet in 1908, however, the jousting ground was London – and it was there that Pound appeared later that year. It was still a time when a brash young talent could sell himself: first to the Regent Street Polytechnic Institute, where he was asked: "Do you want to register as a student?"

"No. I want to register as a teacher. I want to give a course on the Romance Literature of Southern Europe."

"But we don't want a course on the Romance Literature of Southern Europe. And besides, who are you?"

"Let me give the course," said Pound, *"and you'll find out."*

In similar fashion, he sold his second book of poems, *Personae,* to the publisher Elkin Mathews, discoverer of William Butler Yeats. Mathews read *Personae* and told Pound: "If you can make an advance payment on the manuscript, I might consider bringing it out."

"Well," said Pound, *"I've a shilling in my pocket if that's any use to you."*

"No, never mind," said Mathews. "I want to bring the book out anyway."

Mathews did – and it was not long before Pound became what one biographer calls "the innovator to whom all other innovators paid homage"... the poet who caused Yeats to change style in mid-career (a new gauntness, attributable to Pound)... and the translator whom T. S. Eliot called "the inventor of Chinese poetry for our time." It was Pound who arranged the first publication of Eliot's *Prufrock* and who, in 1922, edited *The Waste Land* into what became the most famous poem of the twentieth century. (The original versing, showing Pound's revamping, was published in 1971.) Together, he and Eliot – both of them American expatriates – ruled the world of English poetry for a time.

From London (1908-1921) and Paris (1921-1924) and as "foreign correspondent" of the Chicago-based *Poetry* Magazine, Pound's influence extended to the spheres of letters, music, and fine arts. "As much as anyone, but much earlier than anyone, [Pound] brought Henry James to the fore," one critic has written. Pound has also been described as "one of the discoverers of Vivaldi in our time," and it is because Pound had the Vivaldi works in a Dresden library copied for him that they outlasted their subsequent destruction by Allied fire-bombing. A man of prodigious talents, Pound sculpted and composed music, too – including an opera with words by François Villon and *music* by Ezra Pound. Of this episode, Robert McAlmon reminisces in *Being Geniuses Together:*

> People who had known Ezra for some time did not take his composition abilities with great seriousness, as, so they claimed, Ezra was virtually tone deaf. He was not a trained musician, and it was said that he plunked away at a mandolin or banjo and jotted down notes, seeking a return to the establishing of musical values which the older world had known and which sentimentalized tradition had destroyed.

Nevertheless, when *The Testament of François Villon* was performed at the Salle Pleyel in Paris, McAlmon had to admit that "the singers held our attention far more than most of us had anticipated. Perhaps Ezra *had* caught the right sort of music to suit Villon's poems." T. S. Eliot, however, left early.

Pound crusaded for what he liked – writing whole books extolling the avant-garde music of George Antheil (*Ballet Mécanique*) and the vorticist sculpture of Henri Gaudier-Brzeska. Gertrude Stein particularly disliked *this* side of Pound. She called him "a village explainer, excellent if you were a village, but if you were not, not."

In London, Pound befriended and promoted Robert Frost and railed in 1914 at why *"If there are serious people in America, desiring literature of America, literature accepting present conditions, rendering American life with sober fidelity,"* his fellow American had to go to

England to win publication. In Paris, Pound took boxing lessons from Hemingway and edited his first full volume of short stories, *In Our Time*. (*"Hem did not disappoint,"* Pound often said.) It was Pound who arranged publication of James Joyce's *Portrait of the Artist as a Young Man* as a serial in *The Egoist;* who interested Miss Harriet Weaver in becoming Joyce's financial benefactor; and who even (in collaboration with Yeats) applied successfully on Joyce's behalf for a grant from the Royal Literary Fund. And it was Pound who publicly praised D. H. Lawrence, long before Lawrence was known, even though Pound disliked Lawrence personally. *"Detestable man, but needs watching,"* he confided.

Even then, though, Pound's bias was often economic. He saw Eliot's being *"imprisoned in a bank"* job and Joyce's having to *"bother about shillings and pence"* as *"the cardinal crime of an age which sees ill-advised millionaires expend $30,000 for a pamphlet by Poe the starveling and $100-$200,000 for some canvas by the impecunious Rembrandt or Millet or Cézanne."*

This was a valid observation – and, as always, Pound didn't merely espouse his beliefs, he acted upon them. Another of Pound's discoveries in London had been Major C. H. Douglas and his Social Credit movement. By the time Pound had settled in Italy in the mid-1920's, false credit ("the beast with a hundred legs, USURA") had become his root of all evil:

> *Usura slayeth the child in the womb*
> *It stayeth the young man's courting*
> *It hath brought palsey to bed, lyeth*
> *between the young bride and her bridegroom*
> CONTRA NATURA
>
> *They have brought whores for Eleusis*
> *Corpses are set to banquet*
> *at behest of usura.*
> – end of Canto XLV

Pound's economics found fertile soil in fascist Italy, where the "corporative state" and shortcut solutions of Benito Mussolini not only made trains run on time, but gave men more manhood, women more femininity, and many the illusion of renaissance – to all of which Pound was susceptible. He was broadcasting his economic theories by radio from Rome as early as 1935. He revisited America in 1939 to try to see President Franklin D. Roosevelt and *"keep hell from breaking loose in this world."* But FDR did not see Pound; instead, Henry Wallace (then secretary of agriculture) received him.

During this unsuccessful 1939 trip, Pound indicated that he was, for better or worse, in closer and quicker touch with reality than either the "good Germans" of the Hitler years or the avengers who later clamored for Pound to be hanged. He told a literary agent in New York: *"I don't want to roast little babies. I just happen to like the fascist monetary system."*

Pound always insisted that, if he'd had any notion of betraying America, he could have spared himself his misery by taking Italian citizenship upon his return from the U.S. in 1939. But, as Richard H. Rovere wrote in 1957: "He clung to his American passport. It is a matter of record that [after Pearl Harbor] he tried in 1942 to get aboard the last diplomatic train that took Americans from Rome to Lisbon. He was refused permission to board it. He had no choice but to stay. . . ." And therein lies a complex but elusive truth that I will try to unravel before this book is done.

The poet also claimed that, in his shortwave broadcasts to the "home folks" over Rome Radio, *"I was only trying to tell the people of America how they could avoid war by learning the facts about money."* But it takes more than poetic license to justify the language of his May 5, 1942, broadcast:

> *Europe callin'—Pound speakin'. . . The kike, and the un-mitigated evil that has been centered in London since the British set on the Red Indians to murder the American frontier settlers, has herded the Slavs, the Mongols, the Tartar openly against Germany and Poland and Finland. And secretly against all that is decent in America, against the total American heritage. This is my war all right, I've been in it for twenty years—my granddad was in it before me. Ezra Pound speakin'.*

The U.S. authorities called it treason—and he was indicted in 1943. But, to date, the ultimate word is Pound's (in Canto LXXIV) *"that free speech without free radio speech is as zero."*

In the spring of 1945, two Italian partisans knocked on Pound's door with their rifle butts and led him into American custody. Handcuffed to a black accused of rape and murder, he was driven in an open U.S. Army jeep through the streets of Rapallo, his summer hometown, and onward to the Disciplinary Training Center near Pisa. And there the U.S. Army put him in the "gorilla cage," where the soldiers took away his shoelaces and belt to keep him from suicide, but then built a low hedge of spiked netting all around him: Pound considered this an invitation to slash his wrists, which he resisted. *"They thought I was a dangerous wild man and were scared of me. I had a guard night and day. Soldiers used to come up to the cage and look at me. Some of them brought me food. Old Ez was a prize exhibit."* Another GI brought him tar paper, which was his only shield from rain and sun and stockade searchlights. A tin can was his toilet. Held incommunicado, he was allowed no reading matter except Confucius and was told nobody knew where he was. (The official excuse for this barbarity toward a man approaching his sixtieth birthday was that fascists might try to rescue him.) But, in his cage, Pound wrote.

> *Under white clouds, cielo di Pisa*
> *out of all this beauty something must come,*

The fruit of Pound's ordeal, *The Pisan Cantos*, were published while he was in the Washington insane asylum as mentally unfit to stand trial for treason. And *The Pisan Cantos* were awarded America's most prestigious honor for a poet: the Bollingen-Library of Congress Award of $1,000 for "the highest achievement of American poetry" in 1948. Such was the ensuing uproar that the Government bowed out of poet-toasting thereafter and the Bollingen Prize is now awarded by Yale University. But the jurors, though there was dissent among them, stuck to their guns: "To permit other considerations than that of poetic achievement to sway the decision would destroy the significance of the award and would in principle deny the validity of that objective perception of value on which civilized society is based."*

Thus, just as Cervantes and Bunyan may have found greatness in their prison cells, Ezra Pound reaffirmed his in the cage near Pisa and then, in his Washington bedlam, maintained the image that his age demanded. And there he lingered, but seldom languished, until 1958, certified genius and certified madman, playing to the hilt the role of the caged poet. (A 1967 book about him was titled *The Caged Panther.*) Around 1952, halfway through Pound's incarceration, the two young girls (just out of Hunter College) who founded Caedmon

---

*One of the Bollingen jurors, W. H. Auden, remarked to me in 1971, that while on the one hand, "for his crimes Pound may have deserved hanging," on the other hand, "for his *Pisan Cantos* he deserved the Bollingen Prize." Another juror, Karl Shapiro, simply said that he couldn't vote for an anti-Semite, prize or no prize.

Records went to see him in Washington: "We came to Pound, as most people come to Pound's poetry, with uncertainty and a feeling of less than total sympathy." On the lawn of St. Elizabeth's while inmates hooted and nature rustled, Pound let them record him reading – but forbade any issuance during his confinement. He explained:

"Bird in cage does not sing."

It was a wet autumn Wednesday in Venice, 1971 – and Ezra Pound was staying upstairs in Olga Rudge's house, where the electricity had been shut off for the *acqua alta*. "He may come down," she told the photographer and me when, holding a candle, she admitted us toward noon, "but he certainly won't be going out. He's like a cat – or a human barometer: he feels the weather without having to see it or hear it." Spotting my copies of the *Selected Poems* and *Selected Cantos*, which I'd brought for autographing, she said: "Leave them with me and I'll ask him later today or tomorrow. That's what just might start his day off wrong. This kind of weather – with water coming at you from above and below – makes people twittery as sea gulls."

Their ordinary routine called for her to rise early and do the shopping while he stayed in bed until ten or eleven, took an enriched milk drink for breakfast, and then went strolling arm-in-arm with her on the cobblestoned promenade along the Giudecca Canal.* (*"Will I ever see the Giudecca again?"* Pound asked in *The Pisan Cantos*.) When the weather was good, they ate lunch in a restaurant outdoors; otherwise indoors or at home. Then, in the afternoon, a stroll along the other side of Pound's peninsula, beside the Grand Canal.

("and the Canal Grande has lasted at least until our time.")

Later in the afternoon (though sometimes in late morning when

---

*Groping for symbolism, perhaps, when I was first writing about Pound in late 1971, I phoned a friend in Venice and asked her to check with a librarian whether the name of the Giudecca Canal was derived from the Italian word *"giudaico,"* which means "Jewish." She said she thought it was, but the librarian wasn't sure. When he couldn't find an answer readily in his books, he made one phone call and came back in two minutes with this answer: "No, it derives from the word *'guidicati,'* meaning 'the judged' because the island of Giudecca was used as a place of banishment for the murderers of the Doge Pietro Tradonico in the ninth century – and it was used later as a place of confinement, if not a ghetto, for the Jews, which is why many people think it means "Jewish'." My friend thanked him and asked what his source was. "Oh," said the librarian, "I called the one man in Venice who has such information on the tip of his tongue: Ezra Pound." My friend was flabbergasted: "And he spoke to you?!!" The librarian replied: "He always does. I just tell Olga Rudge what I want and Mr. Pound comes right to the phone with the answer."

17

the weather was bad), Pound always sat in his top-floor studio amidst such treasures as the famous bust of him by Gaudier-Brzeska, who died in battle at twenty-four (*"And Henri Gaudier went to it,/ and they killed him,/ And killed a great deal of sculpture"*), and a Max Ernst sea-shell painting of inestimable value standing propped up in a primitive frame of four sticks of wood, hand-hewn and not-quite-joined by Ezra Pound the handyman. And there he sat, perchance to write – with results that Olga Rudge would neither confirm nor deny. Eva Hesse, Pound's German translator and editor of *New Approaches to Ezra Pound,* insisted, however, in a 1971 letter to me:

> When Harry Meacham wrote in his book [*The Caged Panther,* 1967] that the poet's creativity came to an end with his illness of 1959, he was, in fact, entirely right. Practically everything which has appeared in print over the past 12 years was written in 1958 and 1959; all rumors to the effect that he is "still writing" – however near they may come from the horse's mouth – should be taken *cum grano salis.*

On the other hand, the Prague-born Venetian painter Lotte Frumi (whose 1964 portrait of Pound is owned by the Boston Museum of Fine Arts and her 1972 portrait of him by Yale University) told me how Pound rose at five one morning and informed Olga Rudge that he wanted to read some poems. Olga Rudge, who ministered as engineer to Her Master's Voice, fetched the Grundig and Pound read some verse, apparently new, into the machine in a voice so strong that he sounded a good ten years younger. Then he went back to bed. That night, at a dinner party, Olga Rudge – brimming with excitement – played her tape. All listened. Some wept at hearing this firm, virile voice of old making the English language sing again. Only one person didn't react – Pound, who sat by the machine listlessly and disinterestedly.

All Olga Rudge would say to me then about the possibility of present and future writings by Pound was that "he will never write his autobiography. A short essay of his that could be used as biographical notes is coming out in an anthology – but he allowed its publication only on condition that every sentence beginning with the word *I* should be removed."

And now, by midday candlelight, Ezra Pound was so self-effacing that he wouldn't show his face.

"Ezra!" Olga Rudge called up the stairs. "Ezra?" Then: "Ezra,

don't play possum! Do you want to come down or do we go up?"
There was an answering rustle from above and Olga Rudge's tone
became less sharply playful, more endearing. (She called Pound
"Caro!" and *"Caro Carlo!"* sometimes.) *"Caro,* do you want to go
visit Frumi?"

"*No.*"

"How about Liselotte's?"

"*No.*"

"Where do you want to go?"

"*Nowhere.*"

So the rest of us sat downstairs and chatted. An occasional friend
dropped by – to talk about the *acqua alta* and see that Ezra and Olga
had made provisions. And from the visitors one gleaned little
episodes about the latter-day Pound. He liked to play long-drawn-
out chess games with Giorgio Manera, a Venetian lawyer barely half
his age who, like Pound, had had a cataract removed. When Mrs.
Manera asked her husband: "Who wins?," he replied: "I try my best
to let Ezra win – but it's hard." Mrs. Manera told this to Olga
Rudge, who exclaimed: "That's amazing! Ezra tells me *he* tries to
make your husband win because '*poor Giorgio doesn't see very well.*' "

The poet Peter Russell, known as a member of Pound's "inner circle" of friends, warned me to talk about anything but poetry with
Pound:

"I talked poetry and, for two or three years, I got nothing but
silence about anything. Then one day I talked about violence in
Italy – strikes and bombings in Milano; the resurgence of facism. I
told him that the whole country seemed to be running wild and I
hardly dared to pick up the newspaper nowadays without getting
sick.

"Ezra moved his mouth as though he was going to speak, so I
stopped talking. And he did speak: *'Waaall – if a man's
family – have been peasants for a thousand years – for two thousand
years – and you cover their land with asphalt – what can you expect
them to do? They go crazy!* "

Hearing familiar voices of trusted friends, Pound came down the
stairs at a jaunty pace. Today he was wearing sharp-creased gray
trousers, a blue shirt with the top two buttons open, a gray
sleeveless pullover, blue socks, and open-toed slippers. He smiled,
but would not chat. The conversation turned to the sculptor
Gaudier-Brzeska and his hyphenated name. Olga Rudge asked:
"And wasn't his sister named Sophie-Suzanne? Or was it Suzanne-
Sophie?"

No answer from Pound.

"I think it was Sophie-Suzanne. Am I right, Pound?"

No response.

"Ezra, don't be impossible! Blink twice if yes."

Nothing happened.

"Well, then, blink once if no."

Pound blinked twice.

Words came much later, when the others left and Olga Rudge donned topcoat and green bonnet.

"Where you goin'?" Pound asked.

"Just around the corner to get more matches and candles."

"You work much too much."

"Well, I have to do it, Ezra." She invited the photographer to join her on her errand and then turned to me, saying: "I'll leave you alone with Ezra. Maybe it goes better without me."

Pound and I sat in silence. Five minutes. Ten minutes. I talked about social rituals in Louisville, Kentucky, ("After dinner, the men get left alone to make 'men talk' "). This seemed to generate a flicker – of interest or of the candles flanking Pound? It was hard to tell. More silence. Without a click, as in the theatre, the electric lights came on. Ezra Pound blinked. Then he tried to blow out a candle. The flame danced, but did not exit. Pound blew again. And again.

Old age poses many delicate moments. I asked: "May I do it, sir?"

No answer. But he tried again.

On tiptoes (for no apparent reason), I went over to the other candle – the one he wasn't trying to blow out. I looked at him. He didn't nod, but I blew it out anyway. Then he stopped trying. I blew out the other. As with the last night's whistle-and-wink, a certain camaraderie had been established without words, in spite of words. Now even our joint silences were more relaxed.

Still, at the end of such an afternoon and with scarcely a handful of quotes in my notes, I was exhausted by my monologue with Ezra Pound. Pound, on the other hand, wasn't. As soon as the photographer and I had bade him and Olga Rudge good-bye and before we were out of the house, Pound went bounding up the stairs to sit in his studio.

> *O sun venezian*
>   *Thou that through all my veins*
> *Hast bid the life blood run. . . .*
> —"Alma Sol Veneziae"

On Thursday, there was a break in the rain – and Ezra Pound was raring to go out. As the photographer and I presented ourselves, he donned a brown hat, grabbed his walking stick, and put a reddish-brown checked overcoat over the dark red velvet smoking jacket (with two gold buttons), wide green tie, light brown trousers, and high boots that he was already wearing. Olga Rudge pleaded with him to take an umbrella in case the rain resumed (*"Caro Carlo!* Don't be mean"), but he practically skipped over the marble slab in the doorway and was on his way. One was reminded of a vignette in *His Daughter's Book* – of Pound in 1939, emerging from a Fred Astaire movie, and tap-dancing all the way home through the streets of Venice while tellin Olga and Mary to "get nimble."

Olga Rudge handed me a black umbrella and said: "You can hold it over him when it rains, which it certainly will. We're going to our friend Frumi's on the other side of the Grand Canal, so one more thing: in the gondola, you *must* sit down. Because I *make* Ezra sit down. But I know he won't do it if he sees you two standing up."

Then we raced to catch up with Ezra Pound who was striding ahead briskly. We waited briefly for the shuttle gondola – not the ornate, cushioned kind of gondola that plied the tourist trade for $10 (negotiable downward), but the plain black sort that ferried Venetians across the canals for less than a dime a person; you simply left your fifty-lire coin on the rim of the boat. The gondolier warned that *"Il Signor Poeta"* should not use his stick in the boat because the bottom was wet. Pound sat reluctantly, but remained poised to rise even after the photographer and I had obliged Olga Rudge by unchivalrously outracing a lady to the last remaining seat. Olga Rudge restrained Pound from giving the lady *his* seat.

> They will come no more,
> The old men with beautiful manners
> —"I Vecchi" (1915)

On the San Marco side of the Grand Canal, it was raining and I unfurled the umbrella over Pound's head as he hurried through narrow streets and up and down steps of old stone bridges. Oncoming pedestrians lowered their umbrellas or stood aside in deference not to fame, but to age – though one round-faced young Italian froze with the shock of recognition, thereby blocking our way for nearly half a minute. Then the young man removed his hat, bowed, and hugged a wall to allow room. With an imperious wave of the walking stick, Pound passed.

"*Makes no sense traipsin' through this rain,*" he muttered. And when we arrived at our destination – near the Rialto Bridge in a palace where William Dean Howells once resided – he was still saying to himself while his hostess helped him off with his coat: "*Makes no sense at all.*"

The painter Lotte Frumi was a marvelously mutilingual redheaded widow who knew Kafka in the Prague ghetto and who fought back the tears when she showed us her portrait of her husband, Guido, drawn a few hours before he died at age ninety-two a decade before. (Her sister was Gerty Cori, co-winner of the 1947 Nobel Prize in medicine.) A confidante of Olga Rudge's, Mrs. Frumi was a little nervous about a visit from the Great Man. "Mr. Pound always chooses the most uncomfortable seat," she complained – as Pound sat stiffly, his walking stick at attention, on a Spartan wooden chair.

In our hour there, Pound spoke not a word to Mrs. Frumi, though he twinkled and even chuckled once as she told of the tourist gondolier who points her out to his clientele as "Verdi's widow." Pound clearly relished the atmosphere of her palatial studio.

We all lunched in a large, brightly lit and whitewashed restaurant called Raffaele's, where Pound had been eating for years. It was crowded and we had no reservation, but the management welcomed us and moved people around to make room. Still, Olga Rudge was not quite happy: "It's one of our favorite places and they're always very good to us, but even here the way of life is changing. We like to eat our *pasta* and THEN choose our main course, but they want to know the whole meal right away. The world is in such a hurry."

She ordered for Pound a half-portion of *lasagne* and a whole filet of sole – washed down with red wine (which Pound cut with mineral water). While we awaited the food, I tried my luck asking Pound whether all the Beckett in his apartment reflected admiration for the playwright and his sparing eloquence.

"*No,*' said Pound, "*early poems.*"

"Oh, go on, Ezra!" said Olga Rudge, turning then to me: "Ezra likes Beckett's plays, too. We saw Madeleine Renaud in *Happy Days* here – before, I think, she even did it in Paris. Then Ezra had me send for everything of Beckett's. And when we were in Paris, we saw *Endgame* in a theatre that used to be for Grand Guignol. Isn't that perfect? We had heard Beckett was ill, but Ezra dropped a note asking if he could come around and see Beckett. No, he couldn't—because Beckett insisted on coming to see Ezra. Of course, he and Ezra knew each other a little."

"When Beckett was James Joyce's secretary?" I wondered (mistakenly, for Beckett wasn't Joyce's secretary, but a friend who read to Joyce when his eyesight failed).

Ezra Pound answered me: *"I knew Beckett at Joyce's, but didn't know he was his secretary."*

The *lasagne* came and Pound was the first to finish.

"Did you like your *lasagne?"* Olga Rudge asked.

"Too rich," said Pound.

"But you ate it all."

"Too rich and too much."

"Oh, Ezra! It was only a half-portion."

"That was no half-portion."

"Oh, go on! Look, Mr. Levy ordered a whole portion and he still has more on his plate than you had to begin with."

Pound said nothing and concentrated on the restaurant's afternoon bustle. When the sole came, he devoured it. Olga Rudge, as always, asked how he liked it. And Ezra Pound found fault: *"Full of bones."*

This somehow reminded her of "Mr. Eliot's poem that begins: 'My name is Tough.' I've been trying to remember the rest of it for two days now. How does it go, Ezra?"

Pound was little help, except to correct her: *"Not by Eliot. Early American poem that Eliot liked to recite."*

"And how does it go?" she persisted. Struggling to remember, she came up with:

> " 'My name is Tough
> I come from Tough Alley:
> The further down you go,
> The tougher they get. . . .'

"And then what, Ezra? Please, Ezra, what's the last line?"

Ezra Pound bared his teeth, curled his mouth, and snarled:

> *"I come from the last house."*

It was pouring when we left the restaurant, so Ezra Pound and Olga Rudge and I returned via *vaporetto* from San Marco rather than by gondola. At the entrance to their house, Pound balked at crossing the marble slab he'd stepped over so blithely that morning.

"Come on, Ezra! You can do it," Olga Rudge pleaded. "You can step right over it." Finally, he did – and Olga Rudge said: "He makes believe it's difficult because he disapproves of my putting it there." By the time she'd said this, Pound was on his way up the stairs to bed. It had been an exhausting outing and I didn't see him again that day.

The lights were off and sirens were wailing an *acqua alta* alert. Olga Rudge lit a fire, and she and I and the photographer (who had rejoined us after escorting Mrs. Frumi home) sipped cognac and talked. Hers, one could be certain, had not been an easy lot. As a beautiful young girl nearly fifty years earlier and, in the words of George Antheil, "a consummate violinist," she forsook career and ego and status to devote herself to her "*caro Carlo*." She was kept out of sight during his thirteen years of confinement. Even now, for reasons of propriety, she would not allow herself to be photographed with Pound – though such photos were, of course, taken anyway in Spoleto and elsewhere.

We talked about her duties and difficulties while helping her stack books and other ground-floor treasures on high tables – above imaginable *acqua alta* level. During this puttering of ours, she opened a damask napkin and then snapped it shut hastily. In it, though, I glimpsed a copy of Her Daughter's Book.

She saw I saw – and asked what I thought of the book.

I told her what I thought of Princess Mary de Rachewiltz's elliptical style – and this unleashed a ninety-minute confessional of love and anger and disappointment and grief, past and present, that was too private to print in Pound's lifetime. Wringing her hands and frequently interjecting "See what I mean," Olga Rudge showed me what she'd jotted in the margins as she'd read Her Daughter's Book. It was then that it first dawned on me *why* Pound hadn't left Italy in 1942 – and I vowed to look into it further when and if I outlived him. While he was still alive, though, a friend who had acquired the same information (at a different time in a different place) remarked to me: "King Lear had it easy compared to what Ezra and Olga have had from Mary." I was in no position then to weigh these words, but I do know that – as a father with my own hopes for my children – I went away rent by what I'd heard that evening.

> *They tell me to Mirror my age,*
> *God pity the age if I do do it.* ★

★From the long poem "Redondillas, or Something of that Sort," which Pound deleted before publication of his 1911 collection, *Canzoni*.

Early the next day – my last in Venice and the last time I would see Ezra Pound alive – Mrs. Frumi phoned to thank me for listening to Olga: "It's the first chance she's had to speak about Her Daughter's Book to anyone with no allegiances – and I can only tell you that she and Mr. Pound have been undone by the situation."

That same morning, the photographer and I were invited by Pound and Olga Rudge for a farewell visit and a "simple lunch" of spaghetti, Chianti, veal chops, spinach, and coffee. (Instead of the chops, Pound had "veal burgers" – pure chopped veal cooked without butter – which were so good that he had "seconds" and then we consumed his "thirds" and "fourths" as our "seconds.") Maybe it was the sun peering through (unsuccessfully) or the *acqua alta* receding temporarily, but a new warmth pervaded the house. The books I had left for autographing were returned to me with two inscriptions by Ezra Pound certifying that I am "in touch with reality." Pound even obliged the photographer for nearly thirty minutes before muttering *"Basta."*

In talking *at* Ezra Pound that Friday, I refrained from discussing literature, economics, or politics. Knowing that he'd entered college at the age of fifteen, I sought common ground by talking about some problems experienced by my older daughter when she was "skipped" a year ahead in a competitive French *lycée*. This elicited a question – *"Why do you say 'competitive'?"* – and later an observation: *"It doesn't make one wish one had been born later in history."*

Following this up, I asked: "Would you rather have been born earier?"

"It was better in my father's time."

"How? Simpler? Or were they able to work harder at it?"

"Luckier. My father was born too late for the Civil War and too early to get into all the others."

At another point, I was asking Olga Rudge what Norman Mailer's verses were doing on Pound's shelves. She replied: "Oh, he was here a year or so ago and gave that book to us. I personally like his poetry much better than his prose. I don't like novels that seem to be written by the weight. I had heard this Mailer was a wild man and I was a little afraid, but he was on his best behavior. Butter wouldn't melt in his mouth."

She was starting to impersonate a prim Norman Mailer with hands clasped in lap when Pound chimed in: *"Mailer? Nice . . . young . . . fella."*

Olga Rudge told me: "I read his poems to Ezra." Then, to Pound, she said: "And you liked some of them. Do you remember any?"

Pound replied: *"All of 'em."*

Before I went away, I was almost pleased to see that Their Daughter's Book was no longer concealed in a napkin – but stood on a shelf beside her Italian translations of her father's early Cantos.

> *You were praised, my books*
>> *because I had just come from the country;*
> *I was twenty years behind the times*
>> *so you found an audience ready,*
> *I do not disown you,*
>> *do not you disown your progeny.*
>>>> – "Salvation the Second"

As I was checking out of my hotel in Venice, I took a long-distance call – from the Swiss intermediary, who wanted to know if all had gone well. I thanked him for using his friendship and influence and even his person to bring me together with Pound. And, for the first time, he told me candidly why he had done so:

"Ezra Pound couldn't care less, but there are those of us in his circle who think maximum publicity is the biggest gun toward winning him what he deserves: the Nobel Prize! For literature, if not for peace. Now what do you think? Don't you think the world owes Ezra Pound a Nobel Prize?"

I told him that I didn't know whether the world owed Ezra Pound a Nobel Prize, but I did know from experience that we owed it to ourselves to listen to his silences.

THE AGE DEMANDED

> *Non-esteem of self-styled his betters*
> *Leading, as he well knew,*
> *To his final*
> *Exclusion from the world of letters.*

Ezra Pound never won the Nobel. In fact, during the last months of his life, a self-righteous, vindictive world of politics and letters denied him two lesser prizes. In January of 1972, a professor of English at the University of Maine, Carroll Terrell, proposed Pound for an honorary degree – and the premature message to Pound garbled it from a nomination to an election. Pound cabled his acceptance *"WITH GREAT PLEASURE"* only to learn that the suggestion had been withdrawn. "I was personally hesitant about it," university president Winthrop C. Libby explained. "Our existence depends on what the Maine people approve: they elect the legislature, and the legislature approves our appropriations." It was all "a ghastly blunder," said Professor Terrell, who is managing editor of *Paideuma*, "a journal devoted to Ezra Pound," and he later wrote to *Newsweek*:

> Trustees who would like to honor Ezra Pound do not dare to for fear of the national press, which would likely set up a clamor based on falsehood and exploded myths. . . .
>
> Calls I've had from English newpapers have a tone: how can America keep on doing this? On the Continent they shrug their shoulders and say: "The U.S.A.? What can you expect?"
>
> One newspaper wrote, "Universities can do better than give honors to traitors. Some critics say the only crime Pound was guilty of is the crime of writing poetry in the first place." When trustees have to face a phalanx of such sorry wits filled with ignorance, what can they do?

Later, I asked Olga Rudge how Pound had reacted to this "ghastly blunder." She replied succinctly: "Ezra's used to fools rushing in and talking about things that don't yet exist."

That spring and summer in Boston, the American Academy of Arts and Sciences acted out — first in secret and then in public — some of Carroll Terrell's and Ezra Pound's and my own worst fantasies about the American intellectual establishment.

For his towering influence on modern letters, Ezra Pound was nominated to receive the Academy's prestigious 1972 Emerson-Thoreau Medal — a $2,000 annual honor hitherto awarded to Robert Frost, T. S. Eliot, Katherine Anne Porter, Mark Van Doren, Lewis Mumford, Edmund Wilson, John Crowe Ransom, and the eloquent skewerer of Adolf Eichmann, Hannah Arendt. The panel that selected Pound was headed by Leon Edel, biographer of Henry James. Its members were Mumford; writers John Cheever and Lillian Hellman; Pound's publisher, James Laughlin; and professors Louis L. Martz of Yale and Harry T. Levin of Harvard. The two professors and the publisher were the active proponents of Pound, while Mumford was the only dissenter.

When, however, a mail poll of the Academy's twenty-seven-man governing council indicated that Pound would be approved, two leading Academy officials grew so concerned that a special council meeting was called for April 19. Harvard sociologist Daniel Bell led the attack, contending that art cannot be separated from morality and that Pound did not deserve a humanistic award. "If esthetic expression were given autonomy," the argument went, "then the most despicable things, murder or torture, could be done in its name. It leads to horrible behavior. People become animals." After several hours of heated debate, a few minds were changed. The award was vetoed on moral grounds – "because of other aspects of his life." The vote against Pound was 13 to 9, with two abstentions and two absences.

Professing that it wanted to spare Pound's families pain and "in the best interest of Pound's psychological health," the Academy warned those in the know that these events "are not to be disclosed to the public or press." They weren't even revealed to this national honorary society's 2,700 members – all distinguished names from the natural sciences, social sciences, and humanities – until Dr. Jerome V. Lettvin, a former psychiatrist who became professor of biology and electrical engineering at the Massachusetts Institute of Technology, heard about it from a member of the governing council. Lettvin resigned from the Academy and sent the Boston *Globe* a copy of his letter in which he told the Academy: "It is not art that concerns you, but politics; not taste, but special interest; not excellence, but propriety."

O.B. Hardison, Jr., Director of the Folger Shakespeare Library, and Professor Hugh Kenner of the University of California at Santa Barbara also resigned in protest. Kenner pointed out the paradox of his having been honored with membership for writing his book, *The Pound Era*, while Pound himself was not acceptable to the Academy.

In the uproar that followed, Harvey Brooks of Harvard, the Academy's president, dispatched a "confidential" letter to several members, in which he said:

> Some members of the council suggested that with memories of the holocaust so prominent, the award of the Emerson-Thoreau Medal to Pound, with the unavoidable implication that it carry the special approval of life as well as work, would be deeply offensive to many members of the Academy.

Brooks added that "Pound's anti-Semitism and praise of fascism, and his curious social and economic ideas" were facets of his life that the Academy "could not ignore." And one of the thirteen who had vetoed and thwarted the award – a leading scholar who declined to be identified by name – told Robert Reinhold of the New York *Times*: "Ultimately, what counts is the nature of a humanistic society. No one is going to censor [Pound's] poetry, but we do not have to honor him. There is a distinction between forgiving and honoring. I appreciate Pirandello as a playwright, but he was a fascist – I would not invite him to my home."

Elsewhere in the *Times* – in its Sunday *Book Review* – the English-born critic, novelist, and moralist Wilfrid Sheed pointed out that "the Final Solution had not commenced when Pound gave his famous broadcasts, and indeed he spoke explicity against pogroms." Then Sheed went on to answer the quarter-of-a-century-old question of "Does one honor him?" thusly:

> Pound's contribution to letters is towering: he gave his soul for it; and if he is to live out his long life dishonored, I believe he deserves an explanation with some passion in it . . . not a rap on the knuckles. If I were Jewish, I would hate his guts, and I don't love them as it is. But I think it would be the right kind of honor to say so.

Being Jewish, loving Pound's poetry, and admiring his guts, I felt free to ask Olga Rudge how Pound was taking the furor. She replied: "My dear boy, did you really think the world had become any better since 1949? But, if they think it makes any difference to Ezra, no!"

While the old ugliness and new rancor spewed forth all that summer, Ezra Pound sat in his studio one day (the Fourth of July, 1972) penning what must stand as his last word on the subject. It was in the last three of a seven-paragraph foreword to his *Selected Prose 1909-1965*, which was published in 1973:

> *re USURY:*
> *I was out of focus, taking a symptom for a*
> *cause.*
> *The cause is AVARICE.*

This "last word" was probably the last words written by Ezra Pound. For the candle of his long life, honored and dishonored, was not flickering, but dying out. Toward the end, he ate less, function-

35

ed less, and seldom left his bed. By his eighty-seventh birthday – on a foggy Monday, October 30, 1972 – he was too weak to go downstairs to the birthday party in his honor. So the dozen adult guests came up to him – one by one – to pay their respects and, they suspected, their farewells. Liselotte Höhs brought her son, Manfred, and another neighbor, Mary Jane Matz (of *Opera News* and biographer of the Jewish financier Otto Kahn), brought her two daughters, Margaret and Clare, and her son, Carlino, to greet the man they knew only as "Mr. Pound who plays chess with us and used to baby-sit us."

One who was there recalls that Pound was "a little weak, because he hadn't eaten in two days, but otherwise himself. Sitting up in his bed, he looked beautiful – in a pink cover and bathed in a pinkish light. It's the way I always want to remember him."

And another who made the pilgrimage upstairs says: "He wasn't at all tired, but in excellent form, full of humor, and with real warmth in his eyes. We drank his health in champagne, chatted about Monteverdi, and exchanged old memories. Olga wasn't the least worried about him and neither was I."

Downstairs, though, Olga Rudge had her worries. A painter friend had had a cake baked – large enough to hold eight big blue candles for Pound's decades plus eight little blue candles for the additional years "and one to grow on." But one of the small candles didn't work! The one-to-grow-on was hollow.

Olga Rudge hunted high and low for another small candle. There was no *acqua alta* yet, but anyway, the candles set aside for it were too large for the birthday cake. Finally, she located a small pink candle that worked – but, being at least as superstitious as some of the others present, she and they were just a little perturbed by the one pink amidst all of the blue.

Ezra Pound might have been disturbed, too, but he didn't see the whole cake. One slice was put by his bed, along with one glass of champagne – and he forced himself to take a bit and a sip with each guest who came up. One of the last of these visitors recalled that Pound "complained about the champagne and said '*I shouldn't have eaten that cake*,' so I was quite sure he was himself. The next night – or, rather in the very early hours of Wednesday [November 1, 1972], Olga called me from the hospital and said 'Ezra is dead.' "

It was the holiday time of Halloween and All Saint's Day, when Venetians visit their dead and the *vaporettos* to the island cemetary of San Michele charge no fare. Doctors and nurses were almost as scarce as small blue candles and no proper specialist could be found. So it was that, in his final hours, Ezra Pound had been tended by a children's doctor from Milan and a Venetian general practitioner at a hospital that would not have been his first choice.

If the care of the living was perfunctory, the treatment of the dead was worse. Ezta Pound was first laid on a slab in the hospital's cluttered morgue without even a chair for Olga Rudge to keep her vigil by his corpse among corpses. Only when the journalists began calling and the television crews arrived – making what one witness called "a ferocious din, even by Italian standards, so loud I was really afraid it would wake the dead" – did the hospital staff realize it had not just another body on its hands. Pound was moved to a chapel within the building. Old friends arrived, but didn't stay long – and one of them, Lotte Frumi, was actually elbowed out of camera range by a fellow artist who had been unkind to Pound in his lifetime, but now needed to be seen on TV grieving over Pound's death. When Olga Rudge finally returned home, various lawyers and executors were converging to try to remove whatever of Pound's they could from her possession because she had no official status in his legal afterlife.

The service on November 3, in the Palladian Basilica on the island of San Giorgio, was direct and brief – the way Ezra Pound was in his later years – without the traditional black drapes and flowers for which Venetian funerals are famous. His daughter, Mary de Rachewiltz, attended – with her son, Walter, twenty-four, a literary scholar looking like early photos of his grandfather and awaiting conscription into the Italian army. Pound's official widow, Dorothy Shakespear Pound, and their legitimate son, Omar, did not come.

After the Catholic service (Pound considered himself, religiously, a Confucian, but he had close ties with several churches in Venice), four gondoliers, clad in black, rowed the plain chestnut coffin – adorned by a few wreaths and a bronze crucifix – across the wide lagoon to San Michele. There, amidst cypress and laurel trees, with the abbot of St. George's Anglican Church in Venice officiating, Ezra Pound was laid to rest in a secluded grove.

Two days later, Liselotte's son and the Matz children made their own pilgrimage to San Michele Cemetery to light some candles and put some flowers – marigolds and red roses and a yellow one that the Italians call "The Flower of the Dead" – on their old friend's grave. The Matzes' oldest daughter, Catherine, was not there, for she was already studying in the States at Long Island University's Southampton campus. But of all the letters of condolence Olga

Rudge received, Catherine Matz's is the one she cherishes most. In it, the girl tells of finding out the news of Mr. Pound's death by walking into class and finding a fellow student feverishly chalking his own improvised poem on the blackboard:

"EZRA POUND
IS ALIVE
IS ALIVE
IS ALIVE

. . .

IS ALIVE!"

2
"MAKE IT NEW": A PORTRAIT
IN QUOTES

(When a quotation in italics is not otherwise attributed, it is by Ezra Pound.)

"Wal, Thanksgivin' do be comin' round,
With the price of turkeys on the bound."
> — First two (of eight) lines of what is
> believed to be Pound's first published
> poem — in the Jenkintown (Pennsylvania)
> *Times-Chronicle* of November 8, 1902.

" *'Make it new'* was his cry as he went into battle. He sought tautness, compactness, the hard image that both conveyed and, in a sense, was the meaning the poet was after. Every word that was not functional in the line was eliminated. His own poetry . . . had a lyrical and delicate talent, a skillful sense of rhythm and music and a nervous energy that give the poetry a propulsive vigor."
> — Critic Thomas Lask on the New York
> *Times* obituary page, November 2, 1972.

SIR HERBERT READ who, in *The Tenth Muse* (1957), began his essay on Pound by calling him "an alchemist who transmuted the debased counters of our language into pure poetic metal" and ended by describing him as "one of the few men who have talked sense in our time," said in between: "A man who sets out (1908) with the idea that *'no art ever yet grew by looking into the eyes of the public'* is bound to find himself increasingly isolated from the social matrix that insures sanity (which admittedly may be no more than an accepted code of conduct)."

"With the real artist there is always a residue, there is always something in the man which does not get into his work. There is always some reason why the man is always more worth knowing than his books are. In the long run nothing else counts."
> From *P'atria Mia* (1910-1911)

WILLIAM CARLOS WILLIAMS, a twenty-one-year-old medical

student at the University of Pennsylvania, in a letter to his mother, dated March 30, 1904, about his eighteen-year-old friend:

"He, Pound, is a fine fellow; he is the essence of optimism and has a cast-iron faith that is something to admire. If he ever does get blue, nobody knows it, so he is just the man for me. But not one person in a thousand likes him, and a great many people detest him and why? Because he is so darned full of conceits and affectations. He is really a brilliant talker and thinker but delights in making himself just exactly what he is not: a laughing boor. His friends must be all patience in order to find him out and even then you must not let him know it, for he will immediately put on some artificial mood and be really unbearable. It is too bad, for he loves to be liked, but there is some quality to him which makes him too proud to please people."

Letter to *William Carlos Williams*, dated October 21, 1908, from London – about Williams' apologetically tepid reaction to *A Lume Spento*:

"*Good Lord! of course you don't have to like the stuff I write. I hope the time will never come when I get so fanatical as to let a man's like or dislike for what I happen to 'poetare' interfere with an old friendship or a new one.*" Telling Williams that his criticism was worth "*a dozen notes of polite appreciation,*" Pound listed his ultimate aims:

"*1 To paint the thing as I see it.*
2 Beauty.
3 Freedom from didacticism.
4 It is only good manners if you repeat a few other men to at least do it better or more briefly."

WILLIAM CARLOS WILLIAMS describing a 1909 stroll through Kensington with Ezra Pound: "We moved on, he insisting on being one step in advance of me as always. I remember my brother once in the same situation turned and walked off in the opposite direction."

RICHARD H. ROVERE: "He believed with Whitman that American experience was fit and even glorious material for poetry, and what he was at war with when he left this country was that spirit that denied this and tried only for '*Attic Grace*' and the '*classics in paraphrase.*' '*Make it new*' Pound kept saying, from his colloquial rendering of Confucius, and *'Make it American,'* as if he were a booster of home manufactures at a trade fair."

— From "The Question of Ezra Pound" in *Esquire*, September, 1952

"Beautiful, tragical faces,
Ye that were whole, and are so sunken;
And, O ye vile, ye that might have been loved,
That are so sodden and drunken,
                    Who hath forgotten you?"
— From 'Piccadilly."

a Whitmanesque poem that Pound first published in his *Personae* (1909). Of it, his father, HOMER POUND, recalled: "He wrote that when he was just out of college, and I remember his telling me that though he called it 'Piccadilly' he might just as well have called it 'Broad and Lombard' or 'Front and Chestnut' (streets in Philadelphia), for it pictures what is to be seen in every large city everywhere." Of the same poem, Ezra Pound wrote in his autobiographical essay "How I Began" (1913):

"I waited three years to find the words for 'Piccadilly,' it is eight lines long and they tell me now it is 'sentiment'."

From *"What I Feel About Walt Whitman"* (1909)

"From this side of the Atlantic I am for the first time able to read Whitman, and from the vantage of my education and — if it be permitted a man of my scant years — my world citizenship: I see him America's poet. . . .

"He is America. His crudity is an exceeding great stench, but it is America. He is the hollow place in the rock that echoes with his time. He does 'chant the crucial stage' and he is the 'voice triumphant.' He is disgusting. He is an exceedingly nauseating pill, but he accomplishes his mission. . . .

"I honor him for he prophesied me while I can only recognize him as a forebear of whom I ought to be proud. . . .

"Mentally I am a Walt Whitman who has learned to wear a collar and a dress shirt (although at times inimical to both). Personally I might be very glad to conceal my relationship to my spiritual father and brag about my more congenial ancestry — Dante, Shakespeare, Theocritus, Villon, but the descent is a bit difficult to establish. And, to be frank, Whitman is to my fatherland . . . what Dante is to Italy and

43

I at my best can only be a strife for a renaissance in America of all the lost or temporarily mislaid beauty, truth, valor, glory of Greece, Italy, England, and all the rest of it." – In *Selected Prose 1909-1965*

"A Pact"
"I make a pact with you, Walt Whitman —
I have detested you long enough.
I come to you as a grown child
Who has had a pig-headed father;
I am old enough now to make friends,
It was you that broke the new wood,
Now it is a time for carving.
We have one sap and one root —
Let there be commerce between us."
– Entire poem from *Lustra* (1916)

"From an examination of Walt made twelve years ago the present writer carried away the impression that there are thirty well-written pages of Whitman; he is now unable to find them. Whitman's faults are superficial, he does convey an image of his time, he has written histoire morale, as Montaigne wrote the history of his epoch. You can learn more of nineteenth-century America from Whitman than from any of the writers who either refrained from perceiving, or limited their record to what they had been taught to consider suitable literary expression. The only way to enjoy Whitman thoroughly is to concentrate on his fundamental meaning." – From *ABC of Reading* (1934)

Opening of a poem written for his wife, Dorothy:
"Man's love follows many faces.
My love only one face groweth."
– "Canzoni – To Be Sung Beneath a
Window," From *Canzoni of Ezra Pound*
(1911)

"Have just discovered another Amur'kn. Vurry Amur'kn, with, I think, the seeds of grace." – Pound writing about Robert Frost in March 1913.

"Come, let us pity those who are better off than we are.
Come, my friend, and remember

that the rich have butlers and no friends,
And we have friends and no butlers."
　　　　　 — From "The Garret," in the April
　　　　　 1913, issue of *Poetry* and in *Lustra*
　　　　　 (1916)

WILLIAM CARLOS WILLIAMS: "We had a chronic argument going on between us, he and I, over which was the proper objective
for the writer, caviar or bread. I held out for bread, Ezra for caviar.
This went on for years. Finally one day I got a letter from London
saying: bread.

"But that was only a momentary aberration on the part of the
grrrrrrreatest poet drawing breath in our day! And he meant it.
That was no joke to Ezra. He really lived the poet as few of us had
the nerve to live that exalted reality in our time."

"O God, O Venus, O Mercury, patron of thieves,
Lend me a little tobacco-shop,
*　or install me in any profession*
Save this damn'd profession of writing,
*　where one needs one's brains all the time."*
　　　　　 — Last stanza of "The Lake Isle," from
　　　　　 Lustra (1916)

"Tame Cat"
"It rests me to be among beautiful women.
Why should one always lie about such matters?
I repeat:
It rests me to converse with beautiful women
Even though we talk nothing but nonsense.
*　The purring of the invisible antennae*
*　Is both stimulating and delightful."*

"The Encounter"
"All the while they were talking the new morality
Her eyes explored me.
And when I arose to go
Her fingers were like the tissue
Of a Japanese paper napkin."

"The Bath Tub"
"As a bathtub lined with white porcelain,

45

When the hot water gives out or goes tepid,
So is the slow cooling of our chivalrous passion,
O my such praised but-not-altogether-satisfactory
lady."

> – Three complete poems from *Lustra* (1916)

"Dear Margaret: What the ensanguined lllllllllllllll is the matter with this BLOODY goddamnblastedbastardbitchbornsonofaputridseahorse of a foetid and stinkerous printer??????

"Is his serbo-croatian optic utterly impervious to the twelfth letter of the alphabet????

"JHEEZUSMARIA JOSE!!! Madre de dios y de dios del perro. Sacrobosco di Satanas.

"OF COURSE IF IF IF bloodywell IF this blasted numero appears with anything like the one twohundredand fiftieth part of these errors we are DONE. . . ."

> – 1917 letter to Margaret Anderson of
> *The Little Review* about typographical
> errors in galley proofs of his poems

"Go, my songs, to the lonely and the unsatisfied,
Go also to the nerve-racked, go to the enslaved-by-convention,
Bear to them my contempt for their oppressors,
Go as a great wave of cool water,
Bear my contempt of oppressors."

> – A stanza of "Commission," from *Lustra* (1916)

"He is like a man who goes hunting hedgehogs with bare feet – and finds his prey all prickles; to vary and mix the metaphor, he sits on his little hill in Kensington as if it were the Olympian, casting forth winged words which, like boomerangs, are returned unto him an hundredfold! In the melee his work is disloyally attacked, his least errors are exposed with a malignant triumph; his sensitiveness, which he hides under a cover of bluster, is denounced as a conceit; his fineness of perception is misunderstood as triviality. His scholarship, with its rather overwhelming pretension, is suspect; his polemics verge on hysteria. His fault is that he is an anachronism. With the enthusiasm of a Renaissance scholar, one of those whose fine devotion but faulty learning revealed to the fifteenth century world the civilization of Greece, he lives in an age which looks at literature as a hobby, a freak, a branch of education;

but never as a life study, as a burning passion." – Richard Aldington in *Poetry*, July, 1920

T. E. LAWRENCE ("Lawrence of Arabia") writing to Robert Graves after a 1920 meeting with Pound: "Pound has spent his life trying to live down a family scandal – he's Longfellow's grand-nephew." In one respect, Lawrence's shaft may not have been too far off target: Ezra Pound was related, on his mother's side, to Henry Wadsworth Longfellow. Fifteen years later, in *Jefferson and/or Mussolini*, Pound recalled a meeting with Lawrence: *"I saw Arabian Lawrence in London one evening after he had been with Lloyd George and, I think, Clemenceau. . . . He wouldn't talk about Arabia, and quite naturally he wouldn't talk about what had occurred in the afternoon. But he was like a man who has been chucked in a dungheap and is furtively trying to flick the traces of it off his clothing."*

WILLIAM CARLOS WILLIAMS: "I could never take him as a steady diet. Never. He was often brilliant but an ass. But I never (so long as I kept away) got tired of him, or, for a fact, ceased to love him. He had to be loved, even if he kicked you in the teeth for it (but that he never did); he looked as if he might, but he was, at heart, much too gentle, much too good a friend for that. And he had, at bottom, an inexhaustible patience, an infinite depth of human imagination and sympathy. Vicious, catty at times, neglectful, if he trusted you not to mind, but warm and devoted – funny, too, as I have said. We hunted, to some extent at least, together, and not each other." – From the 1951 *Autobiography* of the poet-physician

ERNEST HEMINGWAY on Pound in his posthumously published memoir of Paris in the 1920's, *A Moveable Feast*: ". . . here was the man I liked and trusted the most as a critic then, the man who believed in the *mot juste* – the one and only correct word to use – the man who taught me to distrust adjectives as I would later learn to distrust certain people in certain situations. . . ." Earlier, in his 1925 "Homage to Ezra," Hemingway wrote astutely: "He tries to advance the fortunes, both material and artistic, of his friends. He defends them when they are attacked, he gets them into magazines, and out of jail. He loans them money. He sells their pictures. He arranges concerts for them. He writes articles about them. He introduces them to wealthy women. He gets publishers to take their books. He sits up all night with them when they claim to be dying and

47

witnesses their wills. He advances them hospital expenses and dissuades them from suicide. And in the end a few of them refrain from knifing him at the first opportunity."

For example, Pound pushed and crusaded for the avant-garde composer *GEORGE ANTHEIL*—blasting Antheil's way into the right salons and even writing a book, *Antheil and the Treatise on Harmony*. Yet Antheil, in his autobiography, *Bad Boy of Music*, wrote that "from the first day I met him Ezra was never to have even the slightest idea of what I was really after in music. I honestly don't think he wanted to have. I think he merely wanted to use me as a whip with which to lash out at all those who disagreed with him. . . ."

Antheil remembered Pound as "a Mephistophelian red-bearded gent . . . in a green coat with blue square buttons . . . and his red pointed goatee and kinky red hair above flew off from his face in all directions." The composer described Olga Rudge as "a dark, pretty Irish-looking girl, about 25 years old, and, as I discovered when we commenced playing a Mozart sonata together, a consummate violinist."

"Pound talks like no one else. His is almost a wholly original accent, the base of American mingled with a dozen assorted 'English society' and Cockney accents inserted in mockery, French, Spanish, and Greek exclamations, strange cries and catcalls, the whole very oddly inflected, with dramatic pauses and *diminuendos*. It takes time to get used to it, especially as the lively and audacious mind of Pound packs his speech—as well as his writing—with undertones and allusions."—Iris Barry (poet, later curator of the New York Museum of Modern Art's film collection) in *Bookman*, October, 1931)

" 'I've found the lowdown on the Elizabethan drama,' he said as he vanished beard-first into the rear of the pavillion; he was always finding the lowdown, the inside story and the simple reason why."—Malcolm Cowley in the 1951 updating of his *Exile's Return* (1934), writing about Pound in Paris in the early 1920's, and diagnosing the *Reader's Digest* crackerbarrel philosopher side of Pound.

Late in his life, *JAMES JOYCE* (1882-1941) wrote of Pound:

"Nothing could be more true than to say that we all owe a great deal to him. But I most of all surely. It is nearly twenty years since he first began his vigorous campaign on my behalf and it is probable that but for him I should still be the unknown drudge that he discovered – if it was a discovery." – Quoted by Paul L. Montgomery in a *New York Times* obituary November 2, 1972.

"Willingness to experiment is not enough, but unwillingness to experiment is mere death."

> – From preface to *Active Anthology* (1933), in *Selected Prose* 1909-1965

"One of the pleasures of middle age is to find out *that one WAS right and that one was much righter than one knew at say seventeen or twenty-three."*

> – From *ABC of Reading* (1934)

"It is only after long experience that most men are able to define a thing in terms of its own genus, painting as painting, writing as writing. You can spot the bad critic when he starts by discussing the poet and not the poem."

> – From *ABC of Reading* (1934)

"European civilization or, to use an abominated word, 'culture' can be perhaps best understood as a mediaeval trunk with wash after wash of classicism going over it." – From *ABC of Reading* (1934)

"There are so many things which I, as an American, cannot say to a European with any hope of being understood. Somebody said that I am the last American living the tragedy of Europe." – Quoted in *New York Times* obituary, November 2, 1972

From *HIS DAUGHTER'S BOOK:* "Babbo met me at the station in Bozen and filled that day so that, in retrospect, it remains one of the happiest and most eventful of my childhood. He treated me like a grown-up. And showed me Verona. . . . I was too thrilled with the presents he had brought me: a tiny wristwatch and a pair of new shoes. The wristwatch he chose. In the shoe shop he sat back and told them to bring something beautiful for the signorina. And when I picked a pair of brown suede with a bit of heel, he gave me an approving look and paid and told me to keep them on if I wanted to. After which, how could I keep my eyes off my wrist and my feet for very long!

"Until, that is, on arriving at Calle Querini, Mamile said those shoes were not suitable, too grown-up. She would keep them for herself and get me another pair." – From *Discretions*, by Mary de Rachewiltz.

OLGA RUDGE's reaction, penned in the margin next to this passage in her copy, reads: "Hardly the first thing I'd say to someone coming in the door."

"Make it new, make it new as the young grass shoot."
> — Rendering of Confucius ("renovate, day by day renew"), in *Jefferson and/or Mussolini* (1935)

> *"Tching prayed on the mountain and*
>   *wrote MAKE IT NEW*
> *on his bath tub*
>   *Day by day make it new."*
> — From Canto LIII (*The Chinese Cantos*: John Adams)

In *Jefferson and/or Mussolini*, Pound explains this ideogram as *"the fascist axe for the clearing away of rubbish (left half) the tree, organic vegetable renewal."*

On a 1934 address by Mussolini: *"The more one examines the Milan Speech the more one is reminded of Brancusi, the stone blocks from which no error emerges, from whatever angle one looks at them.*

  "Lily-liver'd letterati might very well exercise their perception of style on this oration."
> — From this letter sent autumn, 1934, to editor of the *Criterion*, London, and used as a foreword to *Jefferson and/or Mussolini* (1935)

> *"Stone cutter is kept from his stone*
> *weaver is kept from his loom*
> *WITH USURA*
> *wool comes not to market*
> *sheep bringeth no gain with usura."*
> — From Canto XLV (*The Fifth Decad of Cantos*, Siena – *The Leopoldine Reforms*, published 1937)

From the ancient Chinese ethics of Mencius (Mang Tsze) as translated by Ezra Pound: *"To treat the needy as criminals is not governing decently, it is merely trapping them."*

"The men of old, wanting to clarify and diffuse throughout the empire that light which comes from looking straight into the heart and then ac-

ting, first set up good government in their own states; wanting good government in their own states they first established order in their families; wanting order in their families they first disciplined themselves; desiring discipline in themselves they first rectified their hearts." — A timeless passage of Mencian wisdom, which Archibald MacLeish (using and acknowledging Pound's rendition) cited in 1973 to make this point: "Free men, if they are really free, really men, rule themselves, meaning that they rule their minds. Mencius, though he lived 2,000 years before Thomas Jefferson and John Adams, put that simple but essential proposition in words Revolutionary Virginia and New England would have accepted and approved," but which MacLeish, then eighty-one, thought today's "Age of Adolescence" might have trouble swallowing. Nevertheless, MacLeish reminded his readers that "it was not their trousers Mencius' citizens looked into, but their hearts."

"Ezra Pound: native of Idaho, graduate of Hamilton College in the class of 1905, poet, critic, and prose writer of great distinction. Since completing your college career you have had a life full of significance in the arts. You have found that you could work more happily in Europe than in America and so have lived most of the past thirty years an expatriate making your home in England, France, and Italy, but your writings are known wherever English is read. Your feet have trodden paths, however, where the great reading public could give you few followers – into Provencal and Italian poetry, into Anglo-Saxon, and Chinese. From all of these excursions you have brought back treasure. . . . Your Alma Mater, however, is an old lady who has not always understood where you are going, but she has watched you with interest and pride if not always with understanding. The larger public has also been at times amazed at your political and economic as well your artistic credo, and you have retaliated by making yourself – not unintentionally perhaps – their gadfly."
— Citation with honorary degree (Doc-

tor of Letters) awarded by Hamilton College in Clinton, New York, 1939

An unpublished poem, circa 1939, about Franklin D. Roosevelt:
"Our louse of a President stands for Jewry,
All Jewry and nothing but Jewry.
Broadcast on Rome Radio December 7, 1941 (Pearl Harbor Day) about England:
"Ay, ay, sir, where is it? Did the . . . King save it? He did not. Did the Goldschmitts save it? They did not. Does Churchill endeavor to save it? He does not. I repeat, the rot and stink of England and the danger to her empire are from the inside and have been from the time of (the formation of the Bank of England in 1694) *and no number of rabbis and bank clerks in Wall Street and in Washington can do one damn thing for England save to let her alone. And a damn pity they didn't start doing so sooner. That is, a pity for England. . . . Roosevelt is more in the hands of the Jews than Wilson was in 1919."*

After making this broadcast, Pound dropped in on his friend, United Press correspondent Reynolds Packard, and found out that "the U.S. is at war! . . . If you stay, you'll be a traitor." To which Pound replied: *"I consider myself a one-hundred-per-cent American and patriot. I am only against Roosevelt and the Jews who influence him."*

His next broadcast was on January 29, 1942.

ANNOUNCER: "Rome Radio, acting in accordance with the fascist policy of intellectual freedom and free expression of opinion by those who are qualified to hold it, has offered Dr. Ezra Pound the use of the microphone twice a week. It is understood that he will not be asked to say anything whatsoever that goes against his conscience, or anything incompatible with his duties as a citizen of the United States of America."

"Ezra Pound again speaking, speaking from Europe. Pearl Arbor Day, or Pearl Harbor Day, at twelve noon I retired from the capital of the old Roman Empire – that is, Rome – to Rapello to seek wisdom from the ancients. I wanted to figure things out. I had a perfectly good alibi if I wanted to play things safe. I was and am officially occupied with a new translation of . . . Confucius. I have in Rapallo the text of Confucius . . . and the text of the world's finest anthology, namely that which Confucius compiled from earlier authors . . . (And ideograms) *of extreme beauty. Thousands of poets have looked at those hills and despaired. There are points at which some simple ideogram, that is, the Chinese picture world, is so used . . .* (as) *far as our human sense of eter-*

*nity can reach. There is one of the sunrise that I despair of ever getting
. . . to meet it. There was to be* (words lost in transmission, but
possibly: *a change in my) situation.*

"*That is to say, the United States has been for months . . . illegally at
war through what I considered to be the criminal acts of a President
whose mental condition was nht, so far as I could see, all that could or
should be desired of a man in so responsible a position or office.*"

Around that time, Pound was writing in Italian:

"*Fascio*"

"*A thousand candles together blaze with intense brightness. No one candle's light damages another's. So is the liberty of the individual in the
ideal and fascist state*"

and equating "Rome" with "Love" in a palindrome addressed to
Italians.

ROMA

O   M

M   O

AMOR

— Both from Money Pamphlet
November 4 (*A Visiting Card*), published in Italian in Rome, 1942, and later
in English by Peter Russell, 1952, in a
translation by John Drummond

GEORGE ORWELL: "Some time ago, I saw it stated in an
American periodical that Pound only broadcast on the Rome radio
when 'the balance of his mind was upset,' and later . . . that the
Italian Government had blackmailed him into broadcasting by
threats to relatives. All this is plain falsehood. Pound was an ardent
follower of Mussolini as far back as the 1920s, and he never concealed it. He . . . accepted a professorship from the Rome Government
before the war started. I should say that his enthusiasm was essen-
tially for the Italian form of fascism. He did not seem to be very
strongly pro-Nazi or anti-Russian, his real underlying motive being
hatred of Britain, America, and 'the Jews.' His broadcasts were
disgusting. I remember at least one in which he approved the
massacre of the East European Jews and 'warned' the American
Jews that their turn was coming presently."

In fairness to Pound and in view of the fact that Orwell's condem-
nation has occasionally been used in a demagogic way against
Pound by intellectuals, its context should be emphasized. Orwell's

commentary appeared in *Partisan Review* (May, 1949), as part of a *defense* of Pound's winning the Bollingen Prize. Orwell began: "I think the Bollingen Foundation were quite right to award Pound the prize, if they believed his poems to be the best of the year, but I think also that one ought to keep Pound's career in memory and not feel that his ideas are made respectable by the mere fact of winning a literary prize."

The ending of Canto LXXXI, which Cambridge literary scholar George Steiner calls "the greatest piece of modesty and humility since the Book of Job":
"What thou lovest well remains,
        the rest is dross
What thou lov'st well shall not be reft from thee
What thou lov'st well is thy true heritage
Whose world, or mine or theirs
        or is it of none?
First came the seen, then thus the palpable
    Elysium, though it were in the halls of hell,
What thou lovest well is thy true heritage
What thou lov'st well shall not be reft from thee
The ant's a centaur in his dragon world.
Pull down thy vanity, it is not man
Made courage, or made order, or made grace,
    Pull down thy vanity, I say pull down.
Learn of the green world what can be thy place
In scaled invention or true artistry,
Pull down thy vanity,
        Paquin pull down!
The green casque has outdone your elegance.
'Master thyself, then others shall thee beare'
    Pull down thy vanity
Thou art a beaten dog beneath the hail,
A swollen magpie in a fitful sun,
Half black, half white
Nor knowst 'ou wing from tail
Pull down thy vanity
    How mean thy hates
Fostered in falsity,

Pull down thy vanity,
Rathe to destroy, niggard in charity,
Pull down thy vanity,
    I say pull down.
"But to have done instead of not doing
        this is not vanity
To have, with decency, knocked
That a Blunt should open
    To have gathered from the air a live tradition
Or from a fine old eye the unconquered flame
This is not vanity,
    Here error is all in the not done,
all in the diffidence that faltered."
                    — From *The Pisan Cantos*

Last three of a four-paragraph report by four psychiatrists (three for the U.S. Government and one, Dr. Muncie, for the defendant) on Ezra Pound to Chief Justice Bolitha J. Laws, U.S. District Court, Washington, D.C., dated December 14, 1945:

"The defendant, now 60 years of age and in generally good physical condition, was a precocious student, specializing in literature. He has been a voluntary expatriate for nearly forty years, living in England and France, and for the past 21 years in Italy, making an uncertain living by writing poetry and criticism. His poetry and literary criticism have achieved considerable recognition, but of recent years his preoccupation with monetary theories and economics has apparently obstructed his literary productivity. He has long been recognized as eccentric, querulous, and egocentric.

"At the present time he exhibits extremely poor judgment as to his situation, its seriousness and the manner in which the charges are to be met. He insists that his broadcasts were not treasonable, but that all of his radio activities have stemmed from his self-appointed mission to 'save the Constitution.' He is abnormally grandiose, is expansive and exuberant in manner, exhibiting pressure of speech, discursiveness, and distractibility.

"In our opinion, with advancing years his personality, for many years abnormal, has undergone further distortion to the extent that he is now suffering from a paranoid state which renders him mentally unfit to advise properly with counsel or to participate intelligently and reasonably in his own defense. He is, in other words, insane and mentally unfit for trial, and is in need of care in a mental hospital.

"Respectfully submitted,
Joseph L. GILBERT, M.D.
Marion R. KING, M.D.
Wendell MUNCIE, M.D.
Winifred OVERHOLSER, M.D.

WILLIAM CARLOS WILLIAMS (1883-1963), in a letter to Pound's biographer Charles Norman – first published in the New York newspaper *PM* of November 25, 1945, and later used as "Exhibit A" in U.S. District Court, Washington.

"I can't write about Ezra Pound with any sort of composure. When I think of the callousness of some of his letters during the last six or seven years, blithe comments touching 'fresh meat on the Russian steppes' or the war in Spain as being of 'no more importance than the draining of some mosquito swamp in deepest Africa,' 'Hitler the martyr' and all that – I want to forget that I ever knew him. His vicious anti-Semitism and much else have lowered him in my mind further than I ever thought it possible to lower a man whom I once admired. But that isn't the whole story . . . .

"Ezra Pound is one of the most competent poets in our language, possessed of the most acute ear for metrical sequences, to the point of genius, that we have ever known. He is also, it must be confessed, the biggest damn fool and faker in the business. . . .

"But he always felt himself the superior to anyone about him and could never brook a rival. We accepted it on terms he little suspected, for after all he was and remains in his field, a genius. He just lived on a different plane from anyone else in the world, a higher plane! This gave him certain prerogatives. If he was your friend you just forgave it. We were friends. . . .

"Ezra Pound the consummate poet taken as any sort of menace to America when compared with some of the vicious minds at large among us . . . is sheer childishness. He just isn't dangerous; they are. I am not trying to minimize his crime; it was a crime and he committed it willfully. But under the circumstances and knowing what goes on 'in committee' and elsewhere in our magnificently destined country – I don't think we should be too hard on him. I have thought, in spite of his infantile mental pattern, and still think . . . that as a poet Ezra had some sort of right to speak his mind, such as it had become, as he did. . . .

"It would be the greatest miscarriage of justice, human justice, to shoot him."

On February 13, 1946, a jury retired at 3:55 P.M. and deliberated *for three minutes!*

CLERK OF COURT: Mr. Foreman, has the jury agreed upon a verdict?

FOREMAN OF JURY: It has.

CLERK: What say you as to the respondent Ezra Pound? Is he of sound or unsound mind?

FOREMAN: Unsound mind.

Pound was remanded to St. Elizabeth's Hospital, where he remained for another twelve years.

T. S. ELIOT in *Poetry* (September, 1946): "The opinion has been voiced that Pound's eventual reputation will rest upon his criticism and not upon his poetry. (I have been paid the same compliment myself.) I disagree. It is on his total work for literature that he must be judged: on his poetry, *and* his criticism, *and* his influence on men and on events at a turning point in literature. In any case, his criticism takes its significance from the fact that it is the writing of a poet about poetry: it must be read in the light of his own poetry, as well as of poetry by other men whom he championed. . . . Pound's great contribution to the work of other poets (if they chose to accept what he offers) is his insistence upon the immensity of the amount of *conscious* labor to be performed by the poet. . . . He . . . provides an example of devotion to 'the art of poetry'. . ."

In the same issue of *Poetry*, the editor, *GEORGE DILLON*, introduced new work by Pound thusly: "I am as much surprised as any of our readers to see Pound re-emerging in print. If I am going to be honest, I can do as little about it. . . . This new poem is excellent. I should still publish it if the author were not in a hospital, but in a cell awaiting execution."

In 1945-1946, there was another controversy about printing Pound. Random House was preparing to issue a Modern Library Giant volume: *An Anthology of Famous English and American Poetry*, co-edited by William Rose Benet and Conrad Aiken. But Random House editor *SAXE COMMINS* announced: "Random House is not going to publish any fascist. As a matter of fact, we don't think that Ezra Pound is good enough or important enough to include. If we thought he was, we might have carried him anyway. We just don't think he is."

Commins also announced Random House's intention to print the following note on page 788 of the book:

> "At this point Conrad Aiken included in the Modern Library edition of his anthology, on which the present text is based, the following [12] poems by Ezra Pound. . . . When the publishers insisted on omitting these poems from the present edition, he consented upon one condition: that it be clearly stated in print that his wishes were overruled by the publishers, who flatly refused at this time to include a single line by Ezra Pound. This is a statement that the publishers are not only willing but delighted to print."

When the president of Random House, Bennett Cerf, explored his dilemma in the "Trade Winds" column of *The Saturday Review of Literature*, he received enough protests (142 – vs. 140 reader reactions approving Pound's exclusion from the Modern Library's world of letters), to impel him to restore Pound's dozen poems to the anthology in order to "remove any possible hint of suppression." Cerf later called the brief exclusion "an error in judgment."

LOUISE BOGAN reviewing *The Pisan Cantos* in *The New Yorker* of October 30, 1948:

"Pound's imprisonment in Pisa seems to have brought him back to art and to life. *The Pisan Cantos* shows a new sense of proportion. He begins to feel pity and gratitude, and he begins to smile wryly, even at himself. I cannot think of any other record by an artist or a man of letters, in or out of prison, so filled with a combination of sharp day-to-day observation, erudition, and humorous insight."

Critic and teacher *IRVING HOWE* in the May, 1949, *Partisan Review* debate (same forum from which George Orwell was quoted earlier), after Pound was awarded the Bollingen Prize: "To give Pound a literary prize is, willy-nilly, a moral act within the frame of our social world. To honor him is to regard him as a man with whom one can have decent, normal, even affectionately respectful human and intellectual relations; it means to extend a hand of public fraternity to Ezra Pound. Now a hand to help him when he is down, yes. But a hand of honor and congratulations, no. For Pound, by virtue of his public record and utterances is beyond the bounds of our intellectual life. If the judges felt that he had written the best poetry of 1948, I think they should have publicly said so – but not awarded any prize for the year. . . ."

Poet and Bollingen juror *KARL SHAPIRO* in the same *Partisan Review:* "I voted against Pound in the balloting for the Bollingen Prize. My first and more crucial reason was that I am a Jew and cannot honor anti-Semites. My second reason I stated in a report which was circulated among the Fellows: 'I voted against Pound in the belief that the poet's political and moral philosophy ultimately vitiates his poetry and lowers its standards as literary work.' . . .

"The technical charge of treason against Pound is not our concern, but all artists should stand against this poet for his greater crime against civilization. Let the same charge be laid against Stalinist artists. But even if we claim to be objective perceptionists about it, let us at least ask ourselves whether fascism is or is not one of the 'myths' of *The Cantos*. Who will deny that it is?"

Another Bollingen juror, *KATHERINE ANNE PORTER*, wrote in the New York *Times*, October 29, 1950: "Pound was one of the most opinionated and unselfish men who ever lived, and he made friends and enemies everywhere by the simple exercise of the classic American constitutional right of free speech. His speech was free to outrageous license. He was completely reckless about making enemies. His so-called anti-Semitism was, hardly anyone has noted, only equaled by his anti-Christianism. It is true he hated most in the Catholic faith the elements of Judaism. It comes down squarely to anti-monotheism. . . . Pound felt himself to be in the direct line of Mediterranean civilization, rooted in Greece. . . . He was a lover of the sublime and a seeker after perfection, a true poet, of the kind born in a hair shirt – a Godsent disturber of the peace in the arts, the one department of human life where peace is fatal."

EZRA POUND in St. Elizabeth's: Early 1950's, to a visitor who asked how the Cantos were progressing: *"Wal, y'know, Grampa can't do it all – he's gettin' old. Wal, what I mean to say, Grandpa's burst his spring. Now it's up to your generation to raise the cultural status.*

"All that quotin' from different languages is just the easiest way to show that it's all been said before. If I don't translate . . . wal, the same ideas in English are in the neighborhood.

"It takes a while till you get your bearings – like a detective story – and see how it's going to go. I hit my stride in The Fifth Decad of Cantos [XLII-LI, published 1937].

"You've got to get at least one person in your generation to listen to you. It often happens that a man fails when his friends fail him."

And, one New Year's Day in the mid-1950's, Pound protested against the hospital's telecasting the Rose Bowl game for other patients in the place where his visitors customarily waited for him: *They're trying to bring the intelligence of the people on the inside down to the level of the people on the outside.*

From "The Question of Ezra Pound," by *RICHARD H. ROVERE,* in *Esquire* September, 1952:

"This inmate is one of the great champions and liberators of the modern spirit; he is also a crackpot poisoner of the well of opinion — a political crank who has proceeded from funny-money theories to a full-blown chauvinism. This xenophobe Pound is one of the truly cosmopolitan figures of the century — as the preeminent translator of his time, he has been an heroic builder of bridges to other civilizations; there is, however, a chamber of his poet's soul in which a yahoo dwells — a buckwheat oaf sounding off like a Kleagle of the Klavern or a New York street brawler. . . . This cosmopolitan Pound is a true patriot — he has a love for the United States that is genuine and affecting and that has had a great deal to do with the making of American culture over the last fifty years; yet he has been, since November 26, 1945, under indictment for nineteen separate counts of treason. . . .

"In the world as Pound, in his better moments, wants it, first things would be first, and the first thing about him is that he is a great poet. . . . Poetry is not a horse race or any other sort of competition, and it is silly to argue over which poet runs the fastest, jumps the highest, or dives the deepest. Still, a respectable case could be made out to the effect that the century has produced no talent larger or more fecund than Pound's. Certainly the fit comparisons would be with no more than half a dozen other men who write in English. These, as the Literary Establishment sees the matter today, would be T.S. Eliot, Yeats, Frost (some dissent here, probably), W.H. Auden, and Dylan Thomas; later on, some of these names may be removed and replaced by some from the second rank, such as Wallace Stevens, Robert Graves, Walter de la Mare, Marianne Moore, William Carlos Williams, E.E. Cummings, and Robert Lowell."

Editorial in *Life* Magazine, February 6, 1956:

"An Artist Confined"

"Tokyo Rose got out of jail the other day. This American citizen, who did her considerable best to undermine American morale during World War II, has now finished her sentence as a war criminal.

The Nazi storm trooper responsible for the Malmedy massacre of 1944, General Dietrich, is also out of jail, one of a growing line of commutees and parolees.

"If their crimes can be atoned or forgotten in ten years, attention is surely due the case of Ezra Pound, who has been incarcerated for the same length of time. His prison is St. Elizabeth's in Washington, the federal hospital for the insane. He is confined, with the consent of his lawyer, to avoid a treason trial for which he is mentally unfit. He is fit to work on his Chinese translations (he is one of the best translators of poetry who ever lived), to receive friends and disciples, and to reiterate the political and economic nonsense (a weird and ineffectual mixture of Social Credit and anti-Semitism) which he broadcast for Mussolini during the war. . . . Pound's room at St. Elizabeth's has been called 'a closet which contains a national skeleton'."

In 1958, *ROBERT FROST* took the initiative and spoke out for his old mentor: "None of us can bear the disgrace of our letting Ezra Pound come to his end where he is. It would leave too woeful a story in American literature." Frost said he was also acting on behalf of other writers including John Dos Passos, Van Wyck Brooks, Marianne Moore, Carl Sandburg ("They ought to let him out now. He's had enough."), W.H. Auden, T.S. Eliot, Archibald MacLeish, and Ernest Hemingway ("Will gladly pay tribute to Ezra, but what I would like to do is get him the hell out of St. Elizabeth's"). Their petition was supported by a recommendation from Dr. Winfred Overholser, superintendent of St. Elizabeth's (and one of the four psychiatrists who'd recommended Pound's commitment in 1945), that the indictment be dismissed and the poet released to his wife's custody because he would never be competent to stand trial, being "permanently and incurably insane," and would otherwise die insane in St. Elizabeth's.

FROST: "I went down to the Attorney General's office and said 'I'm here to get Ezra Pound out.' They saw I was going to sit until they did something about it – and they did."

U.S. attorney general *WILLIAM P. ROGERS:* "Is there any point in keeping him there if he never can be tried?

Asked about Frost's efforts upon his release in April, 1958, Ezra Pound snapped: *"He ain't been in much of a hurry."* He sailed for Italy and, after giving a fascist salute in Naples harbor, he announced: *"All America is an insane asylum."*

GIORGIO BOCCA, an Italian journalist who covered Pound's landing in Genoa, asked the poet, in print, this rhetorical question: "How is it that you who merited fame as a seer did not see?"

Poet *TOM SCOTT*: "I predict that the next century will see, even be dominated by, a dialogue between the U.S. and China in which Pound's poetry will take on an importance and weight not obvious at the moment: that not only has he woven a new wholeness, or at any rate potential wholeness, out of European and American, but also of Chinese elements." – In *Agenda*, volume 7, number 2, spring, 1959(!). Then, in 1965, Scott wrote again, in Noel Stock's *Perspectives*, a "Festschrift" honoring Pound on his eightieth birthday.

"I disagree with much of his detail in his vision of finance-capitalist society, but not with his general view, and I applaud his caring about such things. Whatever 'side' one is on . . . Pound has made it possible for poets to write about history and the things that really matter socially, and impossible to confine themselves ever again to moonshine and mountain daisies. Morality is a matter of economic behavior, and the poet's concern with human values begins with money and worth, though it may end in New Jerusalem. Pound is unhappy to wake up to find himself on the side that made Belsen; but I am unhappy to have been on the side that made Dresden and Hiroshima and Nagasaki. Let us forgive the past and get on with the job."

Critic *IRVING HOWE* in *World* Magazine, 1972: "Ezra Pound summed up in his career the wrenching contradictions of modernist culture. He was a generous man committed to murderous ideology. A midwestern provincial let loose in the inferno of twentieth-century Europe, he pretended – with an arrogance too many other writers of his generation shared – to universal knowledge on every thing from Chinese culture to economics and began to preach in verse and prose grandiose schemes for monetary reform that were marked by a simplistic illiteracy. His mind contained large amounts of historical information, but he had no ordered sense of European history – small wonder he could be taken in by a buffoon like Mussolini or suppose Stalin to be 'simplehearted.' *The Cantos*, with their linkage of Jefferson and Mussolini, their absurd celebration of Martin van Buren, their rantings against the Rothschilds, are a junk shop of intellectual debris. . . . Yet there are also superb passages in *The Cantos*, brilliantly recorded dialogue, keen fragments of action, affecting lyrics. It is a work of that distinctly American type, the Crank as Genius – or near-Genius."

After Part 1 of this book appeared, in slightly shorter form, as the cover story in the New York *Times* Sunday *Magazine* of January 9, 1972, the author and his editors received the following letters, among many others:
  "So at 86 Ezra Pound is enjoying third helpings of veal and is silent. Why didn't you ask him whether he enjoyed contributing, by his writings and broadcasts, to the murder of six million innocent Jews some very *young*? As a teacher for 45 years when I look at a beautiful brilliant Jewish child in one of my French classes at Stuyvesant High School and I think of all the brilliant Jews destroyed by the Nazis, all the intellectual contributions of a people not even one per cent of the world's population, I grieve. I don't give a damn about Ezra Pound's cantos and his influence on poetry. I think only of his influence on *MURDER*! Too bad they ever let him out of St. Elizabeth's or that *CAGE*! That is where he belongs: in a CAGE. With a name like Levy, how could you visit him and say nothing about his influence on the MURDER of 6 million Jews! Just for a lousy article that is soon forgotten? You should be ashamed of yourself!"
  – Letter to the author from Morris Goodman, Bronx, New York

"METICULOUS, MERETRICIOUS
MULTILINGUAL WORD MECHANIC
OBLONG, SQUARE, ROUND
EZRA POUND.

"VITRIOLIC TRUMPETER
PHILOSOPHIES HITLERIAN – YES
MENTALLY DISTURBED – I GUESS
CONSCIENCE, EMPATHY, COMPASSION, POET
NOBEL PRIZE MATERIAL?
MULTILINGUAL NO.

"P.S. HE'S DONE HIS WORK BOTH GOOD AND EVIL
HE'S HAD IT NICE AND PAID THE PRICE
REST IN PEACE EZRA POUND
NO NOBEL PRIZE, PLEASE."
                    – Poem addressed to the author by

Hiram Gray on an invoice letterhead
of the Sanre Garage in Harlem.

"Ezra Pound is no looser (*sic*), i.e., no Christ. The exquisite irony
is that he may yet outlive all who tried and *failed* to crucify him.
That's the glory of the Artist: He endures. That's the meaning of his
thunderous silence: A silence which echos (*sic*) down the corridors
of time, to sound against every pillar of philistine paltry power that
exists, the thundering trumpet of the Artist's defiance."
— Letter to the editor of the New York
Times Magazine. From J. Scott Free,
Writer, of Naugatuck, Connecticut.

"E.P."
1885-1972

"For a long while you
were owned by everyone,
an object, an
enemy, someone to
defend or excoriate;
owned but not sold
you said come my
songs we will sing
of perfections we
will get ourselves
hated; you said every
day as the sun rises
make it new; you even
said a long time ago
we elect either knaves
or eunuchs to lead us;
you were talking of
america; you were
not a nice man; you
taught us all the
language and you
reinvented the forms;

you lived these last
years in silence, telling
us something more; you
walked naked all your
life putting your
self on the line for
the taking, you were
bought, owned, now
you are dead and in
the perfect way of
this world, now
only the poets can
own you, barter
your brilliance in
their lonely rooms,
parlay your winnings,
fight over your
coat you never once
turned, now the
world is done with
you and only
the poets own you."
— Poem by Joel Op-
penheimer in the November
9, 1972 *Village Voice*, New
York City
It also appears in *'Names,
Dates & Places'*
(St. Andrew's Press, 1978).

3
EXPERIENCING EZRA POUND

To read Ezra Pound is to enter into conversation with him. For the whole of Pound's work is a dialogue between himself and that imaginary listener he addressed so fiercely all his life. You are about to become that listener, so brace yourself for the fireworks that lie ahead.

As with any good conversation, you can begin at the beginning or you may join it wherever it happens to catch your ear. My personal recommendation would be to begin with the paperback edition of his *Selected Poems*, skipping for the time being the excellent 1928 introduction and 1948 postscript by T.S. Eliot and plunging right into the essential Pound, presented chronologically. Here you will meet the whey-faced and lanky, lonely and frightened kid poet – just before he went off to a Europe he already knew from his reading of Robert Browning and Provencal troubadours. He will tell you, with insecure arrogance, in a prefatory note to an early poem called "Na Audiart," that *"Anyone who has read anything of the troubadours knows well the tale of"* a bard's unrequited love for the Lady Audiart, of whom Pound wrote with bittersweet romantic passion shortly after the turn of the century:

> *Though thou well dost wish me ill,*
> > *Audiart, Audiart,*
> *Where thy bodice laces start*
> *As ivy fingers clutching through*
> *Its crevices,*
> > *Audiart, Audiart,*
> *Stately, tall and lovely tender*
> *Who shall render*
> > *Audiart, Audiart,*
> *Praises meet unto thy fashion?*
> *Here a word kiss!*

Then follow him on to Europe – and the classic bombast of his first major poem, "Sestina: Altaforte," with its vigorous, slashing first line ("Damn it all! all this our South stinks peace!") hammered home by tag lines of such eloquent red meat as "Bah! there's no wine like the blood's crimson!" and "May God damn for ever all who cry 'Peace!'" Reading it, one can see and hear Pound performing it aloud for the first time at a Soho restaurant in 1909 – so loudly that the management placed a screen around the poet's table to protect the ears of its bourgeois clientele.

As early as then, one could find the subtle marriage of mood and manner, brilliantly flashy phrasing, and compactness of color that are hallmarks of all Pound's poetry. One early critic, Herbert S. Gorman, noted: "There is always the creation of an atmosphere, always the melody of phrasing, always the quick ear for the shy felicities of beautiful words, always the varying of form to suit the emotional content."

Unfortunately, the *Selected Poems* do not include Pound's other important poem of those days, his "Ballad of the Goodly Fere" – which presents Jesus as *"no capon priest,"* but *"a man o' men"* and *"a mate of the wind and sea./If they think they ha' slain our Goodly Fere/They are fools eternally."* No matter, for it is perhaps Pound's most anthologized poem – and you will come across it in many places, from Bartlett's to Oscar Williams. (It was even reprinted in *The International Sunday School*). And, if you later read Pound's revealing 1913 article, "How I Began" (which can be found reproduced in Noel Stock's anthology, *Perspectives,* but not in Pound's *Selected Prose*), you will catch a glimpse of how he wrote his famous ballad and the trouble he had publishing it:

. . . In the case of the "Goodly Fere," I was not excited until some hours after I had written it. I had been the evening in the "Turkish Coffee" café in Soho. I had been made very angry by a certain sort of cheap irreverence which was completely new to me. I had lain awake most of the night. I got up rather late in the morning and started for the (British) *Musuem with the first four lines in my head. I wrote the rest of the poem at a sitting, on the left side of the Reading Room, with scarcely any erasures. I lunched at the Vienna Café, and later in the afternoon, being unable to study, I peddled the poem about Fleet Street, for I began to realize that for the first time in my life I had written something that "everyone could understand," and I wanted it to go to the people.*

The poem was not accepted. I think The Evening Standard was the only office where it was even considered . . .

until Ford Madox Ford (then named Hueffer) printed it in his *English Review* three months later. Later, reflecting on its success, Pound observed: *"Having written this ballad about Christ, I had only to write similar ballads about James, Matthew, Mark, Luke and John and my fortune was made."*

Now move on through the years and the pages – and across the

Channel – to a two-line poem called "In a Station of the Metro." Pound's account of how he wrote it (also from "How I Began") is many times longer than the poem itself:

For well over a year I have been trying to make a poem of a beautiful thing that befell me in the Paris Underground. I got out of a train at, I think, La Concorde and in the jostle I saw a beautiful face, and then, turning suddenly another and another, and then a beautiful child's face, and then another beautiful face. All that day I tried to find words for what this made me feel. That night as I went home along the rue Raynouard I was still trying. I could get nothing but spots of color. I remember thinking that if I had been a painter I might have started a wholly new school of painting. I tried to write the poem weeks afterwards in Italy, but found it useless. Then only the other night, wondering how I should tell the adventure, it struck me that in Japan, where a work of art is not estimated by its acreage and where sixteen syllables are counted enough for a poem if you arrange and punctuate them properly, one might make a very little poem which would be translated about as follows:

"The apparition of these faces in the crowd:
Petals on a wet, black bough."

And there, or in some other very old, very quiet civilization, someone else might understand the significance.

Still writing about "In a Station of the Metro" and seeking to define with precision the important poetic movement, Imagism, that it epitomized, Pound said later, in his 1916 memoir of the sculptor Gaudier-Brzeska:

All poetic language is the language of exploration. Since the beginning of bad writing, writers have used images as ornaments. The point of Imagism *is that it does not use images as ornaments. The image is itself the speech. The image is the word beyond formulated language.*

The Oriental economy of Pound's imagism attracted the attention of Mrs. Mary McNeil Fenollosa, widow of an American (1853-1908) who had gone to Japan in 1878 as a professor of economics and left there in 1890 as imperial commissioner of arts. At a time when Japan was westernizing even more frantically than it did in our time, Ernest Fenollosa defended the arts of the East and mastered Chinese and Japanese languages and literature. Pound later wrote of Fenollosa:

It may be an exaggeration to say that he has saved Japanese art for Japan, but it is certain that he had done as much as any one man could have to set the native art in its rightful preeminence and to stop the ape-

ing of Europe. He had endeared himself to the government and laid the basis for a personal tradition. When he died suddenly in England the Japanese government sent a warship for his body, and the priests buried him within the sacred enclosure at Miidera.

For more than five years since her husband's death, Mrs. Fenollosa had been looking for a writer to whom she could entrust Fenollosa's sixteen notebooks on Far Eastern literature, including draft translations of Chinese poetry and Nō dramas. Her husband had wanted his treasure to be treated as living literature, not ancient linguistics. Pound's pure, direct images told her that she was near the end of her quest. Between 1913 and 1915, she gave Pound the notebooks plus a free hand to edit and publish anything therein plus the right to any profits plus "£40 to go on with." And Pound embarked upon a new sea of poetry, a study of the Chinese language, and a lifelong preoccupation with the Chinese word-picture.

Thus, a dozen pages of the *Selected Poems* take us on a journey from a station of the Metro to the wonders of *Cathay*, which is where, Eliot contents, Pound invented Chinese poetry for our time. (In his translations of Japanese Nō plays, Pound was to inspire a new dramatic phase in Yeats.) Even as we travel through the final excerpts from *Lustra* (which precedes *Cathay* and includes "In a Station of the Metro"), we find Pound experimenting with his new materials in "After Ch'u Yuan," Liu Ch'e," "Ts'ai Chi'h," "Ancient Wisdom, Rather Cosmic," and a couple of "Epitaphs":

"Fu I"

> *"Fu I loved the high cloud and the hill,*
> *Alas, he died of alcohol."*

"Li Po"

> *"And Li Po also died drunk.*
> *He tried to embrace a moon*
> *In the Yellow River."*

And then we are in *Cathay*, subtitled *"For the most part from the Chinese of Rihaku, from the notes of the late Ernest Fenollosa, and the decipherings of the Professors Mori and Ariga."* To show the magic that Pound wrought, let me quote from both Fenollosa's rendition of Rihaku (which isn't in the *Selected Poems*):

(If you) ask me how much I regret the parting,
I would answer that my sorrow is as much as the
    falling flowers of spring
Struggling with one another in a tangle.
Words cannot be exhausted
Nor can the feelings be fathomed
So calling to me my son I make him sit on the ground
    for a long time
And write to my dictation
And sending them to you over a thousand miles we
think
      of each other at a distance.

and Pound's "Exile Letter" (which is in the *Selected Poems* and ends thusly):

> *And if you ask how I regret that parting;*
> *It is like the flowers falling at Spring's end*
>   *Confused, whirled in a tangle.*
> *What is the use of talking, and there is no end of talk-*
> *ing,*
>   *There is no end of things in the heart.*
> *I call in the boy,*
> *Have him sit on his knees here*
>   *To seal this,*
> *And send it a thousand miles, thinking.*

Read on through *Cathay* and into the next part, more "Poems from *Lustra*" – heeding an admonition Olga Rudge gave me when I visited her in Venice in November, 1973: "Pick up Ezra wherever you want to read him and, when you can't, skip it and go on. Always remember that you're reading Ezra for pleasure."

Whether you are skipping or reading every word, I suggest you pause before the six-page poem, "Mouers Contemporaines." You are about to meet Mr. Hetacomb Styrax, a married virgin of twenty-eight whose *"ineptitudes have driven his wife from one religious excess to another"* and, in the same cast of characters, *"the old men with the beautiful manners"* – and then you plunge right into *Hugh Selwyn Mauberley* (1919-1920), which is Pound's last important stage preceding the Cantos. Of *Mauberley*, T.S. Eliot writes in his introduction, which it is now time to read before confronting more Pound:

> This seems to me a great poem. On the one hand, I perceive that the versification is more accomplished than that of any other of the poems in this book, and more varied. I only pretend to know as much about versifying as my carpenter knows about woodwork, or my painter knows about distemper. But I know very well that the apparent roughness and näiveté of the verse and rhyming of *Mauberley* are inevitably the result of many years of hard work: if you cannot appreciate the dexterity of "Altaforte" you cannot appreciate the simplicity of *Mauberley.* On the other side, the poem seems to me, when you have marked the sophistication and the great variety of the verse, verse of a man who knows his way about, to be a positive document of sensibility. It is compact of the experience of a certain man in a certain place at a certain time; and it is also a document of an epoch; it is genuine tragedy and comedy; and it is, in the best sense . . . a criticism of life.

Reading Eliot's fifteen-page introduction, you will find a loving critical assessment of the Pound you have just read – and now you will have some credentials and power to agree or disagree with a first-rate piece of criticism. You will also find Eliot's reasons for omitting another major Pound poem, *Homage to Sextus Propertius* ("I was doubtful of its effect upon the uninstructed reader, even with my instructions") – along with directions as to where to find it (also available in Part 4 of this book) and "Ballad of the Goodly Fere" ("it has a much greater popularity than it deserves, and might distract some readers from better work of the same period"). And, just in passing, you will have read what criticism should be, but rarely is.

Now, reopen the *Selected Poems* to "Moeurs Contemporaines," but it still isn't time to start reading it just yet. Repair to wherever you can *hear* volume 1 of Caedmon's two-disc recording of *Ezra Pound Reading His Poetry* back in the 1950's in Washington. Virtually all of Pound deserves to be read aloud – and while this can sometimes be difficult without a reading knowledge of Chinese or Greek, who was better equipped than Pound himself?

Let the eye follow (in the pages of *Selected Poems*) what the ear absorbs (from side 1 of the *first record*). Soon after Mr. and Mrs. Hetacomb Styrax, you will meet the poet himself, as a newcomer dazzled by inbred European sophistication, in an episode called "Soirée":

Upon learning that the mother wrote verses,
And that the father wrote verses,
And that the youngest son was in a publisher's office,
And that the friend of the second daughter was undergoing a novel,
The young American pilgrim
Exclaimed:
"This is a darn'd clever bunch!"

It is funny to read; it is hilarious to hear in Pound's crackerbarrel folksnarl.

Then read and listen onward – as the poet renders his own words with a Talmudist's singsong, a Yankee's quaver, and an Irish bard's formal flawlessness of pronunciation. You are no longer just reading Ezra Pound, you are experiencing him. In an eloquent digression ("Cantico del Sole," which you will not find in the *Selected Poems*), you may be swept up by the passion with which Pound intones:

"The thought of what America would be like if the classics had a wide circulation troubles my sleep!"

... and then repeats, with variation:

"The thought of what America, the thought of what America, the thought of what America would be like if the classics had a wide circulation troubles my sleep."

And, then, a few lines later, he returns to these words with:

"The thought of what America, the thought of what America, the thought of what America would be like if the classics had a wide circulation – oh, well – it troubles my sleep."

You can find this poem in the New Directions edition of *Personae*, but you might almost rather not – because the world-weary *"oh, well"* that climaxes it makes it one of the most haunting folk ballads ever heard. Spoken in Washington by a man who had already endured so much and kept not just his sanity, but his vision, intact, it still has the power – after many hearings – to break one's heart anew.

No time for sorrow, however, as Pound charges forward into *Hugh Selwyn Mauberley*. And we learn, in the very first poem of this sequence not only that Pound is Mauberley and Mauberley is Pound, but also how he sees himself:

> *For three years, out of key with his time,*
> *He strove to resuscitate the dead art*
> *Of poetry; to maintain the "sublime"*
> *In the old sense. Wrong from the start—*
> *No, hardly, but seeing he had been born*
> *In a half-savage country, out of date;*
> *Bent resolutely on wringing lilies from the*
> *acorn;*

This first poem, in five parts, that goes on for eighty-eight more lines, is titled "E.P. Ode pour l'Election de Son Sepulchre" ("Ezra Pound, Ode on the Occasion of Choosing His Burial Place"). It was more than half a century premature, just as Pound's dating of his struggle against the tides of his times had been going on for more than three years (he was in his early thirties when he began writing *Mauberley*). He concedes this almost a dozen lines later, toward the end of the poem's first part, when *"unaffected by the march of events"* Mauberley *"passed from men's memory"* in what Pound calls, in French, *"the thirtieth year of his age."* And then, having pronounced his subject dead, Pound rages at what *"the age demanded."*

E.P.'s opening ode to *Mauberley* is much, much more, however, than merely self-pitying self-eulogy. It evolves into a dissent against academic stuffiness and editorial venality; expands into a protest against shoddiness in every phase of human activity; and then explodes as a lament for the dead of World War I:

> *There died a myriad,*
> *And of the best, among them,*
> *For an old bitch gone in the*
> *teeth,*
> *For a botched civilization.*

Analyzing this passage, Professor M.L. Rosenthal—in his excellent *Primer of Ezra Pound*—points out that:

> Much of the work of contrast is done through
> an alliterative device, the linking of words
> beginning in b. First there is the word "best"
> to suggest the youthful dead themselves, and
> then, in angry machine-gun bursts the words

for a rotten society — "an old bitch gone in the teeth," "a botched civilization. . ."

And, a couple of lines later, what else did they die for?

> *For two gross of broken*
> *statues,*
> *For a few thousand battered*
> *books.*

Then Pound doubles back to make his case in detail. The Victorian surge of English philistinism and the consequent neglect of the more abrasive arts are limned so telegraphically in the next two poems that it usually takes "the Ezra Pound industry" (as Olga Rudge calls the academics who grind Pound down to pedantic pancakes) at least a chapter to "explain" two poems of less than a page's length apiece. The suggestion here is simply to relax and enjoy the names and sounds and news that wash around you as Pound reads them — which you can do much more pleasantly *without* having researched to discover that Pound's "Monsieur Verog" is actually Victor Pfarr, the biographer of Ernest Dowson. You don't even have to know who Dowson was (the tubercular romantic poet who "cried for madder music and for stronger wine" and coined such other memorable phrases as "faithful in my fashion" and "gone with the wind") to appreciate M. Verog's telling Mauberley that *"Dowson found harlots cheaper than hotels."*

There is a brief limning of "Brennbaum," a modern, assimilated Jew, and then Pound's scathing portrait of "Mr. Nixon" — not the one who was President of the United States when Pound died, but an unctuous forerunner of today's Big Money Writers who, amidst such wisdom as *"accept opinion"* and *"don't kick against the pricks,"* tosses off, almost as an afterthought:

> *'And give up verse, my*
> *boy,*
> *There's nothing in it.'*

This is on the record. Perhaps the loveliest portion of *Mauberley* is not. This is the "Envoi" that concludes his 1919 work on the poem. Modeled after the song that Henry Lawes made of "Go, lovely rose," Edmund Waller's seventeenth-century poem, Pound's 1919 "Envoi" begins:

> *Go, dumb-born book,*
> *Tell her that sang me once that song of*
> *Lawes:*

and weaves a garland of love and roses *(". . . in magic amber laid,/Red overwrought with orange and all made/One substance and one color/Braving time")* that conjures up Shakespeare's sonnets – or Pound at his tenderest.

The record flows into the 1920 *Mauberley* and, after a while Pound's reprise of what "The Age Demanded" – but this time spelling out Mauberley's prophetic *"final exclusion from the world of letters."* When the recording ends six stanzas later with yet another, highly unlikely, epitaph for Mauberley/Pound –

> *I was*
> *And no more ex-*
> *ist;*
> *Here drifted*
> *An hedonist*

– you may well be as exhausted as that side of the recording, though the poet (according to two who were there in Washington when it was being made) was raring to go on.

At your convenience, finish the *Seleted Poems* (the rest of which is largely early work that Pound rejected for an earlier anthology, but which Eliot liked); make a note of which volumes (*Lustra, Cathay,* etc.) you think you might like to read in full later on; and then leave Pound alone for at least a day or two. You need time to mull, to absorb, to ponder all that heady wine and blood and roses before you confront the *Cantos.*

There is an excellent paperback volume of *Selected Cantos* – the selection having been made by Pound himself in 1965 – but I suggest you use the more complete, hardback 1975 printing of *The Cantos,* containing numbers I through CXX, though numbers LX-II and LXXIII are missing. (These are the "Mussolini Cantos" written by Pound in Italian during World War II and sent to the fascist dictator with a note from the poet saying *"Duce, my talent is at your service."* In 1973, Professor Duilio Susmel announced in Florence that the two missing Cantos were among captured Mussolini papers now in the hands of the U.S. Government and that he had been given photocopies by a former U.S. Intelligence agent. Professor Susmel, an Italian historian who has written fifteen books about

Mussolini and makes no secret of his admiration for him, said he would offer them for publication by the highest bidder. He also said: "They are rather long, and their Italian is nearly perfect.")

Do not tackle the *Cantos* head on. If you have read my little book up to this point, then I suspect you may find yourself most involved in *The Pisan Cantos* (numbers LXXIV through LXXXIV, an apparent distance of one hundred twenty-five pages) – and it is with this self-contained, autobiographical, and historically controversial sequence that you should begin the *Cantos*.

No sooner have you begun than you are presented with the bad end that Pound's hero Mussolini came to: hanging with his mistress Clara

> *by the heels at Milano*
> *That maggots shd/eat the dead bullock*

And Pound himself is in a cage near what is now Pisa's international airport, on the road to Viareggio, not far from the leaning tower. He is reminiscing – and many of the threads and characters of the seventy-three Cantos that have gone before swim in his mind's eye. But he is in touch with the reality that is trying to destroy him *("Till was hung yesterday for murder and rape with trimmings")* even as he turns to memories of Hemingway and Antheil, Adams and Jefferson, Cocteau and Confucius, the nymph of the Hagoromo and Genji at Suma, to sustain him in his ordeal. He remembers Venice and imparts the news that Florian's café in the Piazza San Marco has been refurbished – along with such current events as V-J Day *("I heard it in the s.h. a suitable place/to hear that the war was over")* and Churchill's defeat at the polls *("Oh to be in England now that Winston's out")*. The second of the Pisan Cantos is a song; the fourth requires two pages of appended "explication" of the Chinese ideograms therein, including the one for dawn in:

> *Bright dawn* 旦 *on the sht house*
> *next day*
> *with the shadow of the gibbets attendant.*
> *The Pisan clouds are undoubtedly various*
> *and splendid as any I have seen since*
> *at Scudder's Falls on the Schuylkill*
> *by which stream I seem to recall a feller*
> *settin' in a rudimentary shack doin' nawthin'*
> *not fishin', just watchin' the water.*
> *a man of about forty-five*
> *nothing counts save the quality of the affection*

Pound's folksy Chinese *("yrs truly Kungfutseu")* wander into *"the Bros Watson's store in Clinton N.Y."* and he remembers the American pianist (part Jewish, the other part D.A.R.) Katherine Heyman, fifteen years his senior, whom he romanced in Venice in 1908.

> *Does D'Annunzio live here?*
> *said the American lady, K.H.*
> *"I do not know" said the aged Veneziana*
> *"this lamp is for the virgin"*

But with it all goes power and wisdom:

> *in limbo no victories, there, are no victories —*
> *that is limbo; between decks of the slaver*
> *10 years, 5 years*

As in the fifth Pisan Canto, which ends:

> *there*
> *are*
> *no*
> *righteous*
> *wars*

Pound says later that the problem after any revolution is what to do with its gunmen. And he proclaims defiantly on one occasion that he has been hard as youth for sixty years — but, another time, he groans *"Oh let an old man rest."* And then, when Zeus lies in Ceres' bosom, we are in Canto LXXXI, with its magnificent ending *("What thou lovest well remains")*.

Read on for two more Cantos and then stop just before the last Pisan Canto (LXXXIV, beginning *"8th October"*). This one is also the final selection on the reverse side of the Caedmon record containing *Mauberley*. Play Canto LXXXIV — and only it, for now — while following the text (also available in *Selected Cantos*). The mule Pound mentions was President Franklin Delano Roosevelt; other names like White, Fazio, Bedell — "two Washingtons (dark) J and M," Bassier, Starcher, H. Crowder, and Slaughter are the people around him in the Pisa prison compound. And when Pound speaks those familiar words that *"out of all this beauty something must come,"* hear and marvel at the undeniable affirmation with which he utters those last three words more than a decade after they were written — after more than a decade of living in a madhouse.

But these are not yet the final words of *The Pisan Cantos*. In a lower key of *"O moon my pin-up,"* Pound sets out again on his odyssey through names that are as real to him as Slaughter and H.

Crowder and J. and M. Washington, but these are Wei, Chi, and Pi-kan; the traitors Laval and Quisling (both executed in 1945), whose fates Pound must have faced up to; the prophet Micah and "the last appearance of Winston P.M. in that connection"; John Adams, Senator Arthur Vandenberg (the isolationist turned internationalist), and Stalin; and then the ultimate reality: the chill of day-to-day endurance expressed by a man who already dwelled in eternity:

If the hoar frost grip thy tent
Thou wilt give thanks when night is spent.

Once your own exhaustion from *The Pisan Cantos* is spent, you can go either of two recommended routes:

If you are as interested in the poet as his poetry (or in the politics as the poet), then you should next read either a biography or a casebook. Far and away the best of the case histories is *A Casebook on Ezra Pound* (1959), edited by William Van O'Connor of the University of Minnesota and Edward Stone of Ohio University. It is a journalistic, yet academically solid, collection of news clippings, reports, essays, and even letters to the editor *about* Pound during his years of incarceration in St. Elizabeth's. This well-organized scrapbook (subtitled "The Case of Ezra Pound: Pro and Con Selections") gives the feel as well as the flavor of the forces that were loose in those postwar times – particularly in two chapters by witnesses to Pound's ordeal in Pisa: "The Cage," by Robert L. Allen, and "The Background of *The Pisan Cantos*," by David Park Williams. Another high point is a revealing four-page vignette of a couple of visits to St. Elizabeth's – Weekend with Ezra Pound," by David Rattray – followed by a footnote of indignant "rectification" by Ezra Pound.

If the O'Connor-Stone *Casebook* is unavailable, Charles Norman's *The Case of Ezra Pound* is a readable substitute; Julien Cornell's *The Trial of Ezra Pound* is less readable, though it has its merits.

There are two important biographies: *Ezra Pound,* also by Charles Norman, and *The Life of Ezra Pound,* by Noel Stock.

Poet and biographer (of E.E. Cummings, too), Charles Norman was one of the first to take up the cudgels for Pound – in the autumn of 1945 in the liberal New York newspaper *PM.* His interest in Pound never waned, and both the casebook and the biography were not only reissued several times (most recently in 1968 and 1969, respectively), but also meticulously updated by Norman. His biography breathes with both the fire and the chaos of Ezra Pound's life. But it is this chaos that makes Norman's *Ezra Pound* annoyingly anarchic, if not ever unduly difficult, reading. Be prepared, then, to put up with a biography in which the hero doesn't get born until page 236 and for a choppy prose style that habitually interrupts the narrative flow with such pompous but hollow one-line paragraphs as "The soil was ready" and "Her name was Marianne Moore. They did not meet until 1939."

Noel Stock's biography is more formal and scholarly – to my mind, a soundly researched, well-written, and readable job. If there are any faults, well, one *can* hear an occasional scholarly ax being ground by Stock, an Australian poet and critic. But it is highly recommended, particularly to those interested in Pound as a poet; Norman's is more for those interested in Pound as a man.

If *The Pisan Cantos* were your meat and left you hungry for more, then you should skip the biography/casebook stage for now and, after a day or more of rest and reflection, go on with *The Cantos*. (And, if you went the biographical route, you can now rejoin *The Cantos* with a great deal of personal insight.) I would still recommend that you *not* try to read them from Homeric beginning to staggering end. A teacher of mine, who could intone many of the Cantos from memory and with love, once admitted to me:

> I can read *The Cantos* straight through, but then I don't understand them and my mind wanders. If Pound is quoting somebody in French for pages on end, well, even if I understand French, I don't know if it's Léger he's quoting and I may not have seen the Léger painting he's referring to. A passing reference to "Willie" may be to a President of the United States – Harrison? McKinley? Which Willie? And then, when Pound goes into Japanese, Chinese, old Provençal – I can only try to read it. I can maybe understand many lines. Others that I didn't or don't understand keep coming back to me in the oddest places and situations. But there aren't ten people in the world who could read all *The Cantos* with understanding.

When he spoke, Ezra Pound was still living – so maybe now there are no more than nine. Or maybe yet, with immortality, there may one day be millions. But I doubt it.

Either glance through *Selected Cantos* and zero in on the sections that appeal to you or, better still, having played Pisan Canto LXX-

XIV on Caedmon's first record, stay tuned to the three that are on the same side – Cantos I, IV, and XXXVI – and hear them as they sounded to Pound. Follow them in the book (Cantos I and IV are in *Selected Cantos*, if that's what you're using). Listen closely to number XXXVI and enjoy the blithe spirit with which the middle-aged Pound, nearing fifty in Italy when he wrote it, was preparing to play Polonius *("Beautys be darts tho' not savage")* while still the teen-ager that William Carlos Williams described as loving "to be liked, but . . . too proud to please people":

Go, song, surely thou mayest
Whither it please thee
For so art thou ornate that they reasons
Shall be praised from thy understanders
With others hast thou no will to make company.

Go, reader, on to volume 2 of the Caedmon recordings, for it is mostly *Cantos* plus two other poems that are both in the *Selected Poems:* "The Gypsy" and "Exile's Letter," which was discussed and quoted earlier as an example of what Pound did with Fenollosa's translations from the Chinese.

The first two Cantos on Caedmon's volume 2, side 2, are crucial – for they pertain to Pound's grossest dybbuk, Usura. After the powerful Canto XLV *("With usura hath no man a house of good stone"),* Pound lapses into a crotchety Titus Moody whine to ad-lib: *"And so that you don't continually misunderstand: Usury and interest are not the same thing. Usury is a charge made for the use of money regardless of production and often regardless even of the possibilities of production. I now repeat the theme"* in Canto LI. Then the voice regains its passion and power as it swells forth once more to fight its demon.

Also on volume 2 are an excerpt from Canto LXXVI – a Pisan Canto containing the most impassioned weather report you'll ever hear – and, on side 2, virtually all of Canto XCIX: one of the later Cantos that he wrote in St. Elizabeth's. It is a wise Polonius in his seventies that we hear emerging from Lear's madhouse, dispensing wisdom:

> *Laws must be for the general good*
> *for the people's uprightness.*
> *their moral uprightness.*

— — —

The great balance is not made in a day
nor for one holiday only.
The business of relatives is filiality,
a gentleman's job is his sincerity.
Build pen yeh!*
the family profession
It will bring luck out of the air

If you mind your own business they (the
phonies)
will fade out before they have to be druv.
Wang: that man's phallic heart is from
heaven
a clear spring of rightness,
Greed turns it awry
The sages of Han had a saying:
Manners are from earth and from water
They arise out of hills and streams
The spirit of air is of the country

Canto XCIX is perhaps the most remarkable performance by Pound on the record — replete with ad libs about ideograms and the sounds of him making *"paltry yatter"* in Chinese. It also includes such homey wisdom (only a little of which can be found in the one-page excerpt in the *Selected Cantos*) as *"And if your kids don't study, that's your fault."*

With this recorded sampling ended, it is time to read more of *The Cantos*. I still do not recommend reading them chronologically, though you are now as qualified as you'll ever be to do so. But, having looked through the *Selected Cantos* and listened to the recordings, you probably know where your strongest interests lie. To help you find whatever you think you're looking for, the following summary should be useful:

Cantos I-VII establish Pound's identity with Odysseus and set the tone of myth and epic for the poet's lifelong expedition through many centuries of the real world — what Hugh Kenner calls "the image of successive discoveries breaking upon the consciousness of the voyager."

Cantos VIII-XIX show the origins of the modern world in the Renaissance and the victory of the anticreative forces over the

---

*Pen yeh Pound explains a few lines later, is *"a developed skill from persistence."*

humanistic values of Sigismundo Malatesta and others. Cantos VIII-XI are known as the "Renaissance Cantos" while XIV-XVI are the "Hell Cantos" of war and corruption. Cantos XIII and XVII punctuate them with the contrasting serenities of order and paradise.

Cantos XX-XXX reprise the themes of the first two groups and prepare us for Pound's next Great Leap Forward, in

Cantos XXXI-XLI, where – with letters and documents and conversations, real and imagined – Pound equates the principles of the Founding Fathers, Adams and Jefferson, with his own. He shows how the basic principles ingrained in the Constitution were corrupted by the banking interests and begins to make his case for Mussolini as the last (or the first modern) practitioner of the American Dream. In the last of these Cantos, which are known as the "Jefferson-Nuevo Mundo Cantos," we meet Mussolini as Pound met him (for the first and only time) on January 30, 1933, when Il Duce, having been presented with Pound's *A Draft of XXX Cantos,* printed on vellum, glanced at a few passages and remarked in Italian: "But this is amusing."

"Ma qvesto,"
said the Boss, *"e divertente."*
catching the point before the aesthetes had got there;

Cantos XLII-LII make the heart of Pound's case against Usura and thus should not be read without first reading the preceding "Jefferson-Nuevo Mundo Cantos." You will also begin to feel some of the venom, which later evolved into his radio rantings, coming to the fore, though even here Pound makes a distinction among Jews *("poor yitts . . . paying for a few big jews' vendetta on goyim").*

Cantos LIII-LXI are the "Chinese Cantos" with their Confucian essence of "MAKE IT NEW."

Cantos LXII-LXXI are the "John Adams Cantos," wherein we find Pound's American forefather heroes mixing freely with Chinese ideograms and ominous current events of the late 1930's *("Schicksal, sagt der Fuhrer").**

Cantos LXXII and LXXIII are the missing "Mussolini Cantos" written in Italian, that were apparently discovered in 1973. By the time this book is in print, they should be available in their original Italian – and eventually in English, too. Once they have appeared in the Italian translation of the *Cantos,* on which Mary de Rachewiltz was at work for the Mondadori publishers, they would then be included in subsequent English-language editions. Pound was work-

---

* *"Destiny, says Hitler."*

ing on a translation of them and Olga Rudge says there is "no reason at all why they shouldn't be published. They're very fine."

Cantos LXXIV-LXXXIV are the "Pisan Cantos," which you should have read and of which we've spoken – and which, of course, speak for themselves.

Cantos LXXXV-XCV, finished in the Washington insane asylum and first published separately in 1956 as *Section: Rock-Drill*, are a massive, summarizing recapitulation of all that has gone before, promising, as M.L. Rosenthal puts it, "an even fuller revelation than has yet been vouchsafed us of the Earthly Paradise."

Cantos XCVI-CIX, also known as *Thrones*, begin – but only begin to carry out this promise. *Thrones* was published in 1959. Drafts and fragments of the remaining eleven cantos *(CX-CXX)* were issued – largely à la carte in one- and two-canto installments – between 1960 and 1972, the year Pound died.

When Pound first conceived *The Cantos* in 1915, he modeled it on Dante's *Divine Comedy.* It was to be 120 cantos in length – divided into Purgatory, Hell, and Paradise. Yet all three, which he of all men experienced on earth, overlapped and took Pound to many unforeseen places and adventures. Part of his silence during those last years in Italy stemmed from his exhausting wrestle with the problem of finding a "Paradise" with which to end *The Cantos*. Still looking for the vision and the bold stroke that would bring his life's work together, Pound wrote in his 116th Canto:

I have brought the great ball of crystal,
  who can lift it?
Can you enter the great acorn of light?
  but the beauty is not the madness
Tho my errors and wrecks lie about me,
  and I cannot make it cohere . . .

Which is why, on the few occasions when he spoke in those years, he would sometimes complain that something or other *"lacks coherence."* But, toward the end, he exulted that he had found:

SPLENDOUR,
  IT ALL COHERES.
  There is so much beauty,
  How can we harden our hearts?
Do not move
Let the wind speak
  That is Paradise.

(The first two lines about splendor cohering were not new to Pound. They were there in his early 1950's translation of Sophocles'

Women of Trachis, proving, perhaps that there is nothing newer than ancient wisdom.)

These are the barest bones of *The Cantos*. Their meat and flesh await you. Any judgment of Pound's search and fulfillment is yours – and so is the enjoyment of the journey. Pound once described his aim as being *"to write an epic poem which begins 'In the Dark Forest,' crosses the Purgatory of human error, and ends in the light."* Others have described *The Cantos* as Pound's "intellectual diary," "a gigantic work-in-progress," and "the boldest experiment in poetry of the 20th century." Babette Deutsch has written:

> *The Cantos* are like a tremendous tapestry in which certain designs predominate, or like a great fugue with recurrent motifs, or like a modern Commedia, with the stenches from hell more often than not climbing up to smother purgatory and hover cloudily on the sill of paradise. . . . Pound uses . . . stories, some legendary, some apocryphal, some true, to symbolize or exemplify the cruelties of usury, and to point up his fury with those "who set money lust before the pleasures of the senses," those responsible for the mutilation of men and of art. In his rage he sometimes gets out no more than a stuttered curse or lashes blindly at the innocent, but I do not think even Dante has more powerfully set down the hideousness of corruption, and the fewest lyricists have equaled Pound's gift for evoking particulars of breath-taking delicacy and luster.

M.L. Rosenthal urges that you look at each group of Cantos as a "new *phase* of the poem, like each of the annual rings of a living tree." Harold H. Watts, in what is considered a definitive book, *Ezra Pound and the Cantos,* speaks of them, too, in the singular and says: "The poem and its import exist to be weighed and measured not only as poetry but as the particular urgencies felt by a particular man of this century."

Beyond that, you will find little further guidance here. *The Cantos* are the ultimate journey into Pound and the most exalted conversation with him. Your experience will depend on what you bring to it and what you take from him.

After *The Cantos*, you may crave more Pound poems (in which case, read *Collected Shorter Poems* or follow other leads you picked up in *Selected Poems*) or you will want to tackle one of the biographies discussed earlier (Norman's or Stock's) or you are ready to read the prose of Ezra Pound. Or perhaps a play: his translations of Sophocles' *Women of Trachis*, completed in St. Elizabeth's, and *Japanese Nō Plays* are generally available. But, with Ezra Pound, the play is *not* the thing and neither is the prose nor the politics – the poetry is! – so I recommend that, unless you're already en route toward a thesis or an obsession, you limit yourself for now to only one or two or three prose samples.

There are *Literary Essays* and *Polite Essays*; selected letters and collected letters and even *Imaginary Letters*; correspondence with Joyce, Yeats, and William Carlos Williams; *ABCs* of reading and economics; *Indiscretions* and *Instigations*; translations and anthologies. But, wherever your tastes lie, sooner or later you should not miss these three prose works:

ABC of Reading (1934) is not just that, but a basic manual for authors, journalists, and anyone who writes so much as a letter. It should be reread periodically, and it would do you no harm to perform the various literary calisthenics Pound proposes. Rereading it, I always appreciate Pound's admonitions *("Incompetence will show in the use of too many words")* and definitions *("Literature is news that STAYS news"* and *"A Japanese student in America, on being asked the difference between prose and poetry, said: Poetry consists of gists and piths")*. Above all, every paragraph of Pound's *ABC of Reading* is a plea for integrity, and his metaphor is sometimes monetary:

> *ANY general statement is like a cheque drawn on a bank. Its value depends on what is there to meet it. If Mr. Rockefeller draws a cheque for a million dollars it is good. If I draw one for a million it is a joke, a hoax, it has no value. If it is taken seriously, the writing of it becomes a criminal act.*

There are marvelous anecdotes involving Maupassant, Flaubert, and the zoologist Agassiz as well as dissections revealing Pound's preference for Chaucer over Shakespeare, Shakespeare over Milton, and Provençal over German verse. For those wishing to study or write poetry, there is a concluding "Treatise on Meter."

Jefferson and/or Mussolini deserves reading if you still want to know more about the poet, his enthusiasms, his economics, and his frustrations. All are on the surface – right from the copyright page's inscription:

APRIL 1935 . . . FINALLY A FOREWORD
THE BODY OF THIS MS. WAS WRITTEN AND LEFT MY HANDS
IN FEBRUARY 1933. 40 PUBLISHERS HAVE REFUSED IT. . .
through his in-between, prefatory letter to the editor of *The Criterion* in London (autumn, 1934):

> *I fail most lamentably at ten and five year in-*
> *tervals precisely when I attempt to say*
> *something of major interest or importance.*
> *Trifles or ideas of second or third line, I can*
> *always offer in manner acceptable to my editors.*

And, later on in his text, his unwillingness to compromise or talk down:

> *I shall go on patiently trying to explain a com-*
> *plex of phenomena, without pretending that its*
> *twenty-seven elements can with profit to the*
> *reader be considered as five.*

The phenomena are confronted early with Pound's basic question:

> *Nobody can understand the juxtaposition of*
> *the two names Jefferson-Mussolini until they are*
> *willing to imagine the transposition:*
> *What would Benito Mussolini have done in*
> *the American wilderness in 1770 to 1826?*
> *What would Tom Jefferson do and say in a*
> *narrow Mediterranean peninsula containing*
> *Foggia, Milan, Siracusa, Firenze, with a crusted*
> *conservatism that no untravelled American can*
> *even suspect of existing.*

His questions he answers sometimes with aphorisms:

> *Jefferson was super-wise in his non-*
> *combatancy, but John Adams was possibly right*
> *about frigates. Unpreparedness and sloppy*
> *pacifism are not necessarily the best guarantees*
> *of peace.*

And direct comparisons:

> *As to Jefferson's interests, let us say his prac-*
> *tical interests: he was interested in rice, be believ-*
> *ed in feeding the people, or at least that they*
> *ought to be fed, he wasn't averse from pinching a*

> *bit of rice or at least from smuggling a sack of particularly fine brand out of Piedmonte. With the moral aim of improving all the rice in Virginia.*
>
> *Mussolini has persuaded the Italians to grow better wheat, and to produce Italian colonial bananas.*
>
> *This may explain the "Dio ti benedica" scrawled on a shed where some swamps were.*

And at least one notable disclaimer:

> *This is not to say I "advocate" fascism in and for America, or that I think fascism is possible in America without Mussolini, any more than I or any enlightened bolshevik thinks communism is possible in America without Lenin.*
>
> *I think the American system* de jure *is probably quite good enough, if there were only 500 men with guts and the sense to USE it, or even with the capacity for answering letters, or printing a paper.*

Selected Prose 1909-1965 offers the broadest contact with Pound's writings on history, religion, music, poetry, his contemporaries and his Chinese, money, economics, and America. Brilliantly edited and organized by William Cookson, it contains the important preface written by Pound on July 4, 1972 distinguishing once and for all between *USURY* and *AVARICE*. It also contains large doses of Pound's *ABC of Economics* and *Money Pamphlets,* which offer the best exposition of the historical logic behind Pound's "crackpot economic theories." There is even, in this context, a slap at Freud:

> *For every man with an anxiety state due to sex, there are nine and ninety with an anxiety state due to lack of purchasing power, or anticipation of same. It is typical of a bewildered society that it should erect a pathology into a system . . .*

as well as, elsewhere, numerous gists and piths *("Every man has the right to have his ideas examined one at a time")* and one devastating rebuke to his native land, written in Italy in 1927:

> *The dread horror of American life can be traced to two damnable roots, or perhaps it is only*

one root: 1. The loss of all distinction between
public and private affairs. 2. The tendency to
mess into other people's affairs before
establishing order in one's own affairs, and in
one's thought. To which one might perhaps add
the lack in America of any habit of connecting or
correlating any act or thought to any main prin-
ciple whatsoever; the ineffable rudderlessness of
that people. The principle of good is enunciated
by Confucius; it consists in establishing order
within oneself. This order or harmony spreads
by a sort of contagion without specific effort.
The principle of evil consists in messing into
other people's affairs. Against this principle of
evil no adequate precaution is taken by Chris-
tianity, Moslemism, Judaism, nor, so far as I
know, by any monotheistic religion. Many
mystics do not even aim at the principle of good;
they seek merely establishment of a parasitic
relationship with the unknown. The original
Quakers may have had some adumbration of the
good principle. (But no early Quaker texts are
available in this village.)

Pound was hardly immune to his second symptom. In fact, the
key – and perhaps eternal – paradox of Pound as a man has been
stated by Richard Rovere thusly:

> In Ezra Pound's extraordinary person, the
> antipodal qualities clang and clatter, the
> denial crowds the affirmation, antithesis is
> always on the heels of thesis. Throughout his
> life, he has esteemed the Confucian ideal of
> order, and much of his work reflects it; yet his
> life and his work, taken as a whole, are sheer
> chaos – though sometimes a glorious chaos, as
> in what William Butler Yeats called the "stam-
> mering confusion" of the *Cantos*, the most im-
> posing of all his work. This great man has
> stood at once for love and for hate, for friend-
> ship and for misanthropy, for reason and for
> befuddlement, for unexampled purity and for
> pure muck, for luminous spirits like Yeats and

Robert Frost and for deranged ones like
Benito Mussolini and for fanatics. . . .*

The next Pound to confront is the critic. I don't recommend
much tarrying with Pound's critical writings unless you're at least
one-third as well-read as he was. (For critical writing ABOUT
Pound, I commend to you M.L. Rosenthal's *A Primer of Ezra Pound*
and J.P. Sullivan's Penguin Critical Anthology, *Ezra Pound*). There
is, however, one graphic sample of Pound the Critic-&-Editor in action: the facsimile and transcript (on facing pages) of T.S. Eliot's
original manuscript of *The Waste Land* with Pound's massive
revamping marked in pen on the left and printed in red on the right.
From this beautiful volume (published in late 1971), you can see
how, in 1922, Pound transformed the manuscript of a sprawling,
chaotic poem that Eliot titled *He Do the Police in Different Voices* into the most influential poem of modern times. And why Eliot
dedicated *The Waste Land* to "Ezra Pound *il miglior fabbro*," meaning "the better craftsman."

This definitive old-new *Waste Land* also contains an illuminating
chronology by Eliot's second wife, Valerie, and a three-paragraph
preface by Pound, written in Venice in 1969, that begins, *"The more
we know of Eliot, the better. I am thankful that the lost leaves have
been unearthed."*

The most passionate, however, of the many words Pound expend-
ed on Eliot were written after the old "Possum's" death – for the
Sewanee Review in 1966:

> He was the true Dantescan voice – not honored
> enough, and deserving more than I ever gave
> him. . . . Am I to write "about" the poet
> Thomas Stearns Eliot? or my friend "the
> Possum"? Let him rest in peace. I can only
> repeat, but with the urgency of 50 years ago:
> READ HIM.

The advice applies to Ezra Pound, too, and to everybody else you
meet in the pages of his life: Yeats, Eliot, Frost, Henry James, Wyndham Lewis, Ford Madox Ford, D.H. and T.E. Lawrence,
Marianne Moore, Jean Cocteau – the list is infinite. One of the
many dividends of experiencing Ezra Pound is that it offers both excuse and incentive to read or reread *The Waste Land* or
Hemingway's *A Moveable Feast* (containing a chapter on "Ezra

---

*From "The Question of Ezra Pound," in *Esquire*, September 1952

Pound and his Bel Esprit") with fresh eyes or a new view – and, this above all, for pleasure. Remember, please, that there is nothing wrong with reading great men or lesser men for sheer enjoyment.

The one last essence of experiencing Ezra Pound must be "recommended" with mixed and turbulent emotions. It is His Daughter's Book: *Discretions*, by Mary de Rachewiltz, later published in paperback as *Ezra Pound, Father and Teacher: Discretions*. It is certainly the most intimate and revealing book that has been written *about* Ezra Pound – and it probably will be unless Olga Rudge writes a memoir of her fifty years with him.* In the meantime, Her Daughter's Book deserves your attention as the next best, though perhaps the worst, thing. Rereading this oddly written memoir, one thinks in such oxymoronic terms as "bittersweet," "love-hate," "cruel kindness." Yes, there is understanding: Mary comprehends her father's economic theories, and even agrees with some of them, but she recognizes that it was his language which got out of hand when he wrote about Usura. And there is cruelty – as in the scene where Olga appropriates Mary's shoes and another in Venice, where the little girl admits that she wants to go back to the Tyrolean farm family with whom she was wet-nursed and boarded out a few days after she was born.

There is Mary's terrifying account of how, as the Allies landed in Italy in September of 1943, Pound fled on foot from Rome and made his way to Bologna, sleeping in an air-raid shelter, and then by train to Verona, and then to the Tyrol to see his daughter. There are literary revelations-in-passing and an understanding of *The Cantos* that only a daughter/translator who learned them at the poet's knee can bring. But there are also gaps which are anything but accidental – particularly in father's-and-daughter's reunion and ultimate dissolution at her castle, Brunnenburg, all of which Princess Mary glosses over in less than a page of gossamer prose ("But by now we had all had enough of Greek tragedy"). Most notably, daughter Mary doesn't tell *why* her father didn't leave Italy when war was declared on America in December, 1941. And yet a second reading of *Discretions* convinces me that she knows what I now know. But Mary isn't telling, so I think I must.

What went on in the seven and a half weeks between Pound's un-

---

*When I suggested this to her in 1973, she winced and said she was not about "to join the Ezra Pound industry" – but indicated that she might give thought to the idea "after I put Ezra's affairs in order." In 1974, however, she told me she could use "a knight in shining armor" to defend *her* name, though Pound's needs no defending.

wittingly timed Pearl Harbor Day broadcast and his January 29, 1942, return to the airwaves is a chapter his biographers have been forced to straddle. Charles Norman says that "what happened in Pound's case is wrapped in mystery." Noel Stock says that "what happened during the next month or so is not clear" and adds that "I have heard that either early in 1942 or later Pound was prepared to leave by the Clipper but was offered instead a passage on a steamer going to Portugal; this he declined on the ground that it would be too risky. His daughter told me in November 1966 that she remembered him coming to Siena to say goodbye to her and her mother before leaving for America but something prevented his departure. I have also heard that on another occasion both Olga Rudge and his daughter might have gone with him but again something happened." Stock does not specify what.

A lesser biographer, Eustace Mullins, reiterates the tale that Richard Rovere has cited — about Pound being refused permission by a consular official to board the last diplomatic-and-press train from Rome to Lisbon. Perhaps so, perhaps not — but there were still ways for Pound to have left. Why didn't he?

An Italian friend of Pound's, Francesco Monotti, has recalled that the poet made all arrangements to leave. His prized Gaudier-Brzeska drawings and sculpture, his furniture and books and other art were carefully distributed to Italian friends for safekeeping. Monotti has written (in *Il Mare*, October 31, 1954):

> The American Government had notified American citizens scattered around the world, and the Pounds, like good citizens, were ready to obey and return to the United States. But at the consulate there must have been someone who thought of them as black sheep. In those supreme moments between day and night in their lives, something of grave consequence must have happened at the consulate at Rome. . . . He returned a completely changed man. . . . He decided quickly, the tickets were returned to the airline, Ezra Pound decided to remain in Italy.

Which brings us to daughter Mary de Rachewiltz's crucial last words which I've italicized, on the subject:

> And there were dramatic moments and periods of great tension following the news of Pearl Harbor. Babbo went to Rome. When

America officially declared war he stopped
broadcasting over the Italian radio. Im-
pressive envelopes arrived summoning all
American citizens to return to the States, to
get in touch with the Swiss legations. Mamile
seemed at a loss. *And what about me? What,
who, was I?*

Babbo came back from Rome, indignant
and discouraged. They would not allow him
on the last clipper out of Rome. It was reserv-
ed for American diplomats and press envoys.
If he and his family wanted to leave Europe it
would have to be by slow boat. Months on a
route full of mines and torpedoes. "Is that the
way they want to get rid of me?" – I think a
way out was suggested by train to Portugal. I
do not remember details. The words that
stuck in my mind are: clipper, the last clipper,
frozen bank account, Grandfather's U.S.
government pension withheld, the old man in
the hospital with a broken hip.* Mamile's
house in Venice sequestered as alien
property.

"AND WHAT ABOUT ME? WHAT, WHO, WAS I?" Those key
words tell me that Mary has known for some time what I was told
in November, 1971 – and which I swore to keep secret as long as
Pound lived. What follows is what I was told – and what a couple of
other close friends admit to hearing, perhaps from the same source:

*When Pound went to see the consul (in Florence, perhaps, not Rome)
he was told that he and Olga Rudge would be helped to travel back to
the U.S., but not Mary. Despite the emergency, they could not, in a
short time, obtain a U.S. passport for a child born abroad illegitimate-
ly.*

*Pound, at first, was still willing to go. But Olga Rudge refused to
abandon their daughter, even temporarily, to the vicissitudes of
war – with mother and father on one side and their child on the other.
And so Pound didn't go.*

---

*Ezra Pound's father, Homer, had broken his hip falling out of bed and was in no shape to
travel. He died soon thereafter in the Rapallo hospital. Mary de Rachewiltz has, on occasion,
given her grandfather's health, as the reason for her father's staying.

Because of her role in Pound's staying and broadcasting, Olga Rudge contends, to this day, that "if they locked him up they should have locked me up — but they had nothing to lock either of us up for."

"And what about me?" asks the princess Mary. "What, who, was I?" Ezra Pound stayed largely for Olga Rudge's sake, and he stayed partly for the sake of his ailing father, but he also stayed for the love of Mary.

"What thou lovest well remains/the rest is dross." Surely the burden was Mary's, too. And, if the dross of it was a Greek tragedy of Learlike proportions, who else can say that *"nothing counts save the quality of the affection"?* But out of all this horror and recrimination something did come: the best of *The Cantos*.

4
BIBLIOGRAPHY: FROM HAMILTON COLLEGE TO HALLMARK CARDS

How to Use this Bibliography: Numbers atop most titles are Library of Congress call numbers. They are useful not only in libraries that classify books accordingly, but also for the reader who wishes to ascertain, by contacting the Library of Congress, whether or not a certain book is on its shelves in Washington or what libraries elsewhere in the U.S. have it.

Numbers in bold face are Dewey decimal classifications for finding books on most library shelves. Dewey decimal numbers vary from library to library, but the numbers herein should provide you with the basic codes that will help you find specific or related works in most libraries that use the system, though it is wisest to consult a library's own card catalog. *Warning:* Biographical works are often classified by libraries, not under Dewey decimal number 920 (biography), but under B (POU), etc.

Some books – particularly those published abroad and a few (believe it or not!) overlooked by the Library of Congress – have not been cataloged at press time. Other numbers sometimes appearing are International Standard Book Numbers (ISBN) and Library of Congress card catalog numbers. Some details, such as new editions and paperback reprints and prices where listed, are subject to frequent change.

Additional quotations or comments by the author, editors, or cobibliographer are italicized.

A. BY POUND, EZRA LOOMIS, 1885-1972

HB171.7.P58/1953 Rare Bk. Coll.
ABC of Economics. 2d. Tunbridge Wells, Eng. P. Russell, 1953, 74 p.
This is the Pound Press edition. First edition was London, 1933. Faber & Faber. **330.1.** 54-29328.

PN83.P57/1934
ABC of Reading, by Ezra Pound. New Haven, Yale University Press, 1934. xii, 197 p. "The present book is intended to meet the need for fuller and simpler explanation of the method outlined in 'How to Read'." p. ix.
PN59.P6/1960
Also available in New Directions paperback, no. 89, with at least nine printings since 1960; 206 pp., $1.75. **028.** 34-37267. Copyright A 76337.

PS3531.O82A75 Rare Bk. Coll.
Alfred Venison's poems; social credit themes, by the poet of Titchfield Street. London, S. Nott, 1935-. 32 p. (Pamphlets on the new economics, no. 9.) "These poems . . . were edited by A.R. Orage and appeared in the New English weekly between February and November 1934." *Contains this tribute from Ezra Pound, who wrote it under pseudonym: "Only Social Credit could have produced this poet."* (Series.) Alfred Venison, pseud. of Ezra Pound. **811.5.** 37-16503 rev.

ML410.A638P7/1968
Antheil and the Treatise on Harmony, by Ezra Pound. New introd. by Ned Rorem. New York, Da Capo Press, 1968. 16, 150 p. music. (Da Capo Press music reprint series.) "An unabridged republication of the first American edition published in Chicago in 1927." 67-27463/MN.

NB553.B73P66
Brancusi. Versione dall'inglese di Mary de Rachewiltz. Milano, All'insegna dal pesce d'oro, 1957. 15, 19. p. 29 plates. Bibliography: p. 25-26.
A collector's item in the Library of Congress' Italian archives. Pound's Little Review (Autumn, 1921) essay on the sculptor, translated into Italian by his daughter. 1. Brancusi, Constantin, 1876-1957. 59-22730.

THE CANTOS
(Chronologically)

The cantos. Cantos 1-30
PS3531.O82 O29/1974
A draft of xxx cantos, by Ezra Pound. Paris, Hours Press, 1930. 2

p. 1., 7-141, 1 p. 11. 212 copies. "200 copies on Canson-Mongolfier soleil velin M.R.V. paper numbered 1-200. No. 134."

Later published in larger editions, New York, Farrar and Rinehart, and London, Faber & Faber, both 1933. 46-39393, New York, Haskell House, 1974. Franklin Center, PA., Franklin Library, 1980. **811.5**74-6379 and 80-138791.

The cantos. Cantos 31-41
PS3531.0 82E4/1934
Eleven new cantos, XXXI-XLI, by Ezra Pound. New York, Farrar & Rinehart, incorporated, 1934- . 3 p. 1., 3-56p. A continuation of the author's "A draft of xxx cantos" published in 1933.
London edition (Faber & Faber, ltd.) has title: a draft of cantos XXXI-XLI. **811.5.** Copyright A 76431, 34-33650.

The cantos. Cantos 42-51
PS3531.0 82F5/1937a
The fifth decad of cantos. New York, Toronto, Farrar & Rinehart, Inc., 1937- . 3 p. 1., 3-46 p. At head of title: Ezra Pound. Cantos XLII-LI; a continuation of the author's "Eleven new cantos, XXXI-XLI." *London edition by Faber & Faber, same year.* **811.5.** 38-625.

The cantos. Cantos 52-71
PS3531.0 82C27/1940a
Cantos LII-LXXI. Norfolk, Conn., New directions, 1940. 5 p. 1., 3-167 p. At head of title: Ezra Pound. "Notes on Ezra Pound's cantos, structure & metric" signed S.D.: 15 p. in pocket. *London edition by Faber & Faber, same year, slightly more elaborately printed.* **811.5** Copyright. 40-34229.

The cantos. Cantos 74-84
PS3531.0 82P5
The Pisan cantos. New York, New Directions, 1948, 118 p. No. 74-84 of The cantos. *London edition by Faber & Faber, 1949, says: "These . . . Cantos called 'The Pisan Cantos' because they were composed when the poet was incarcerated in a prison camp near Pisa . . ."* **811.5.** 48-4592.

The cantos. Cantos 1-84, collected.
PS3531.0 82C28
The cantos of Ezra Pound. New York, New Directions, 1948, also

London, Faber & Faber, 1954. 149, 56, 46, 167, 118 p. port. CON-
TENTS – A draft of XXX cantos. Cantos LII-LXXI. The Pisan
cantos. Annotated index to The cantos of Ezra Pound; cantos
I-LXXXIV. By John Hamilton Edwards and William W. Vasse,
with the assistance of John J. Espey and Frederic Peachy. Berkeley,
University of California Press, 1957. xiv, 325 p. port., geneal.
tables. 25 cm. PS3531.082C28, Index. **811.5** 48-4633 rev.

The cantos. Cantos 85-95
PS3531.082S4/1956
Section: rock drill, 85-95 de los cantares. New York, J. Laughlin,
1956. 107 p. (A New Directions book.) In English. *First published in
Italy in English, 1955 "Ed. originale, curata da Vanni Scheiwiller;
Milano, Pesce d'oro."* 1956. **811.5.** 56-4113.

The cantos. Cantos 96-109.
PS3531.082T5
Thrones; 96-109 de los cantares. New York. New Directions, 1959,
126 p. Half title: Cantos 96-109 of Ezra Pound. In English. **811.52**
59-123172.

The cantos. Cantos 1-95
PS3531.082C28/1965
The cantos, 1-95 by Ezra Pound. New York, New Directions Pub.
Corp., 1965, 1956. 149, 56, 46, 167, 118, 107 p. port. (A New Direc-
tions book.) CONTENTS. A draft of XXX cantos. eleven new can-
tos, XXXI-XLI. The fifth decade of cantos. Cantos LII-LXXI. The
Pisan cantos. Section: Rock-drill, 85-95 de los cantares. **811.52**
65-27558.

The cantos. Canto 110.
PS3531.;082C25 Rare Bk. Coll.
Canto CX by Ezra Pound. Cambridge, Mass., 1965, 8 p. mounted
front. "Number 37 of an edition limited to eighty copies printed as a
present for Ezra Pound on his eightieth birthday, October 30, 1965,
Cambridge, Massachusetts, U.S.A. as (sic) Sextant Press."
66-84748.

The cantos. Cantos 110-117.
PS3531.082D74 Rare Bk. Coll.
Drafts & fragments of Cantos CX-CXVII by Ezra Pound. New

York, New Directions Pub. Corp., 1968-. 32 p. (A New Directions book) 3.95. *London edition, Faber & Faber, published 1970.* **811.5'2** 69-13585.

The cantos. Selections.
PS3531.082A6/1970
Selected cantos of Ezra Pound. New York, New Directions Pub. Corp. 1970-. 119 p. (A New Directions paperbook, NDP304.) (A New Directions book.) $1.95. *London edition published earlier, Faber & Faber, 1967.* **811'.5'2** 75-114846 MARC.

The cantos. Cantos 1-117. Collected
PS3531.082C24/1970
The cantos of Ezra Pound. New York, New Directions Pub. Corp., Contents. A draft of XXX cantos (1930). Eleven new cantos XXX-XLI (1934). The fifth decade of cantos XLII-LI (1937). Cantos LII-LXXI (1940). The Pisan cantos LXXIV-LXXXIV (1948). Section: Rock-drill de los cantares LXXXV-XCV (1955). Thrones de los cantares XCVI-CIX (1959). Drafts and fragments of cantos CX-CXVII (1969). **811',5'2** 70-117217 MARC.

The cantos. 1-120 completed.
PS3531.082C24/1972   MARC 2
The cantos of Ezra Pound. New York. New Directions Book, 1972-. 803 p. $12.50. ISBN 0-8112-0350-6. *Third printing of 1970 collection, revised to include Canto 120, written in 1969, but dated 1972.* **811'.5'2.** 70-117217.

The Cantos. Revised collected edition.
PS3531.082C29/1975
The cantos of Ezra Pound. London, Faber, 1975. 802 p. **811'.5'2.** 76-3777390.

PS3531.082C35 Rare Bk. Coll.
Canzoni of Ezra Pound. London, E. Mathews, 1 911. viii, 51, 1 p. *(Text in English.) Dedication: "To Olivia and Dorothy Shakespear.":* *his mother-in-law and bride-to-be.* 46-31193.

PS3531.082C3/1913
Canzoni & ripostes of Ezra Pound whereto are appended the com-

plete poetical works of T.E. Hulme. London, E. Mathews, 1913. 4 p. 1, vii-viii, 51, 3 p. 1 1., 7-63, 1 p. 13-21698. PR6031.092C3 1913.

PS3531.082A17
Collected early poems of Ezra Pound, edited by Michael King with an introduction by Louis L. Martz. New York, New Directions, 1976. London, Faber, 1977. 330 p., illus. **811'.5'2.** 76-7086 and 77-375221

PS3531.082P4/1968
Collected shorter poems by Ezra Pound. 2nd ed. London, Faber, 1968. 3-297 p. 30/-. (B 68-14644.) First published in 1952 under title: Personae; collected short poems. **811'.5'2.** 68-118263.

Culture. (see Guide to Kulchur).

PS3531.082Z532
Dk-some letters of Ezra Pound, edited with notes by Louis Dudek. Montreal, DC Books, 1974. ISBN 0-919688-05-5 paperback. 145 p. **811'.5'2.** 75-312652

PS3531.082Z535
EP to LU: nine letters written to Louis Untermeyer by Ezra Pound. Edited by J.A. Robbins. Bloomington, Indiana University Press, 1963. 48 p. facslms. Bibliographical references included in "Notes" (P. 29-46). "Works cited": p. 47-48. **816.52.** 63-9720.

ML60/P925E9
Ezra Pound and music: the complete criticism, edited with commentary by R. Murray Schafer. New York, New Directions, 1977. 530 p., illus. **780'.8.** 77-9609

N7445.2 P675/1980
Ezra Pound and the visual arts, edited with an introd., by Harriet Zinnes. New York, New Directions, 1980. 322 p., 3 leaves of plates, illus. **700** 80-36720

PS3531.082E96/1978
"Ezra Pound speaking": radio speeches of World War II, edited by Leonard W. Doob. Westport, CT, Greenwood Press, 1978. 465 p. **940.53** 77-91288

PS3531.082Z626
Ezra Pound, the London years. Exhibition of materials by Ezra Pound and Dorothy Pound held at Sheffield University Library in 1976. Sheffield, England, Sheffield University Library, 1976. 32 p. Limited edition of 450 copies. **811'.5'2.** 80-464179

PS3531.082E9 Rare Bk. Coll.
Exultations. Poems. London, E. Mathews, 1909. 51 p. *Contains 27 early poems and two pages of reviews of Pound's* Personae *including "This is a most exciting book of poems" (Oxford Magazine) and "A queer little book which will irritate many readers" (The Evening Standard).* I. Title. 49-36622.

NB553.G35P6/1970
Gaudier-Brzeska, a memoir by Ezra Pound. New York, New Directions Pub. Corp., 1970. 147 p. illus., ports. (A New Directions book.) 7.50. Includes bibliographical references *and 30 plates of illustrations. First published in London in 1916 and again in 1939; in U.S., 1961.* **730'.924** 78-107490, MARC.

PS3531.082C8/1952
Guide to kulchur. Norfolk, Conn. New Directions, 1952. 379 p. (Also available in ND Paperback, $2.95.) First American ed. published in 1938 under title: Culture. *With prefatory note: "It is my intention in this booklet to commit myself on as many points as possible" and dedication "To Louis Zukofsky and Basil Bunting strugglers in the desert."* **818.5** 52-12149.

PS3531.082H6/1934
Homage to Sextus Propertius, by Ezra Pound. London, Faber & Faber, ltd., 1934. 3 p. 1., 9-35 p. **811.5** 35-5012.

PN83.P6/1971
How to read, by Ezra Pound. New York, Haskell House, 1971. 55 p. Reprint of the 1931 ed., *a forerunner to* ABC of Reading. **028.** 79-169105. MARC. ISBN 0-8383-1315-9.

PS3531.082H8 Rare Bk. Coll.
Hugh Selwyn Mauberley, by E.P. London, The Ovid Press, 1920. 3 p. 1., 9-28 p. 1 1.
   Initials. Poems. "Edition of 200 copies . . . 15 copies on Japan

vellum numbered 1-15 and not for sale. 20 signed copies numbered 16-35. 165 unsigned copies numbered 36-200. This copy no. 63." 45-22705.

Not classified by Library of Congress, although Olga Rudge insists a copy was sent there, as well as to New York Public Library and British Museum;
If This Be Treason. *Rome Radio talks by Ezra Pound.*
   A book printed in an edition of 300 copies, under Olga Rudge's supervision, while Pound was in St. Elizabeth's Hospital. Designed to show the scope of his Rome Radio talks and put them into perspective, it contains the following: "E.E. Cummings"... "E.E. Cummings examined"... "James Joyce: To His Memory" ... Canto XLV (Usura) with Pound's introduction to his reading of it ... Reminiscences of Blair Magazine.
   Olga Rudge's preface: "These talks are printed from the original drafts. No cuts, corrections, or changes have been made. I have not been able to consult the author about this or other matters . . . ."

PS3531.082I6/1930 Office
Imaginary letters, by Ezra Pound. Paris, The Black sun press, 1930. 2 p. 1., 56 p., 2 1. "This first edition . . . is strictly limited to 50 copies on Japanese vellum numbered 1 to 50 and signed by the author together with 300 copies on Navarre paper numbered 51 to 350 . . . to be sold at the bookshop of Harry F. Marks . . . New York City and at the Black Sun Press, Paris. **327.**" 814.5 32-10881.

E169.1.P69
Impact; essays on ignorance and the decline of American civilization. Edited with an introd. by Noel Stock. Chicago, H. Regnery Co., 1960. xviii, 285 p. Bibliography: p. 284-285. **917.3** 60-10860.

PS3531.082 I 65 Rare Bk. Coll.
Indiscretions; or, Une revue de deux mondes. By Ezra Pound. Paris, Three mountains press, 1923. 3 p. 1., 9-62 p. 1 1. "Three hundred copies . . . printed . . . number 45." *Dedication: "To A.R. Orage, at whose request this fragment was first hitched together."* 44-43075.

PN71.P7 Rare Bk. Coll.
Instigations of Ezra Pound, together with an essay on the Chinese

written character, by Ernest Fenollosa. New York, Boni and Liveright, 1920. viii, 388 p. *Freeport, N.Y. Books for Libraries Press, 1967. Essay Index reprint series.*
CONTENTS: A study of French poets. Henry James. Remy de Gourmont. In the vortex. Our tetrarchal precieuse. Genesis. Arnaut Daniel. Translators of Greek. An essay on the Chinese written character by the late Ernest Fenollosa. 1. French poetry. 19th cent. Hist. & crit. 2. English literature 20th cent. Hist. & crit. 3. Greek literature. Translations. 4. Chinese language. Writing. I. Fenollosa, Ernest Francisco, 1853-1908. II. Title. 20-8532. Copyright A 566890.

JC481.P66/1936
Jefferson and/or Mussolini; L'idea statale; fascism as I have seen it, by Ezra Pound, New York, Liveright publishing corp.; London, S. Nott, 1936. 3 p. 1., v-xi, 11-128 p.
Previous edition in London, S. Nott, 1935; currently available in Liveright U.S. paperback L-13, $1.95, which specifies: "This book is being reissued under a contract which was executed in 1935 and does not necessarily reflect Ezra Pound's present view" **320.1** 36-3936.

PS3531.082Z53
Letters, 1907-1941, edited by D.D. Paige. 1st ed., New York, Harcourt, Brace, 1950. xxv, 358 p.
Also available as New Directions paperback NDP 317, $2.95, under title "The Selected Letters of Ezra Pound" with a preface by Mark van Doren; London edition by Faber, 1951; New York, Haskell House, 1974. **928.1** 50-10346 and 74-11145

PS3531.082Z5513
Letters to Ibbotson, 1935-1952, edited by Vittoria L. Mondolfo and Margaret Hurley, introd. by Walter Pilkington. Orono, National Poetry Foundation, University of Maine, 1979. 145 p., fascime. **811'.5'2.** 78-55724

PN37.P65/1979
Literary essays. Edited with an introd. by T.S. Eliot. London, Faber and Faber, 1954. xv, 464 p. *Available* in U.S. as New Directions paperback NDP 250, $3.25. **804** 54-2976. Westport, CT, Greenwood Press, 1979. 54-2976 and 78-13133.

PS3531.082A6/1965
A lume spento, and other early poems by Ezra Pound. New York, New Directions, 1965. 128 p. facsims. port. "Bibliographical note": p. 124. *New edition of his first published book, Venice, 1908. Also contains "A quinzaine for this Yule," 1909, and some previously unpublished poems from his "San Trovaso" notebook. London ed. by Faber and Faber, 1965-1966.* **811.52** 65-15670.

PS3531.082L8/1973
Lustra of Ezra Pound. New York, Haskell House Publishers, 1973. 115 p. port. Reprint of the 1916 ed. published by E. Mathews, London and Alfred A. Knopf, New York, 1917. Poems.
"Cathay, for the most part from the Chinese of Rihaku [i.e. Li Po] from the notes of the late Ernest Fenollosa, and the decipherings of the professors Mari and Ariga": p. 65-94. *Title page definition: "LUSTRUM: an offering for the sins of the whole people, made by the censors at the expiration of their five years of office."* (Elementary Latin Dictionary *of Charlton T. Lewis.)* **811'.5'2, 72-11762. MARC.**

PN511.P63/1971
Make it new; essays by Ezra Pound. New Haven, Yale University Press, 1935. Republished St. Clair Shores, Mich., Scholarly Press, 1971. vii, 407 p.
"Published on the Mary Cady Tew memorial fund."
CONTENTS: Date line. Troubadours: their sorts and conditions. Arnaut Daniel. Notes on Elizabethan classicists. Translators of Greek. French poets. Henry James and Remy de Gourmont. A stray document. Cavalcanti. **809.** ISBN 0-403-01158-2. 71-145243. MARC.

PL887.F45 Rare Bk. Coll.
with Fenollosa, Ernest Francisco, 1853-1908.
'Noh,' or, Accomplishment, a study of the classical stage of Japan, by Ernest Fenollosa and Ezra Pound. New York, A.A. Knopf, 1917. viii, 267, 1 p. front. (port.). Includes music. 45-42106.

E169.1.P7 Rare Bk. Coll. Copy 2
Patria mia. Chicago, R.F. Seymour, 1950. 97 p. "An essay written before 1913 now published for the first time." *Subtitle: "A Discussion of the Arts/ Their Use and Future in America."* **917.3.** 50-8396.

E168.P86/1962
Patria mia, and The treatise on harmony. London, P. Owens, 1962.
95 p. *A British edition of Pound's lost essay plus a later work (see "Antheil and the treatise on harmony").* 64-31010.

PS3531.082A17/1958
Pavannes and divigations. New York, New Directions, 1958. 243 p.
Illus.
"Collections . . . [of pieces] which have been difficult to obtain for
many years." *Sketches and essays reprinted in part from various
periodicals. Book first published by Knopf, 1918.* **818.5** 58-9510.

PS3531.082P4/1909
Personae [poems] of Ezra Pound. Leondon, E. Matthews, 1909,
viii, 9-59, 1 p. "First published in April, 1909." 10-7307 Revised.
NOT TO BE CONFUSED WITH
PS3531.082P4/1926 Rare Bk. Coll.
Personae, the collected poems of Ezra Pound, including Ripostes,
Lustra, Homage to Sextus Propertius, H.S. Mauberley. New York,
Boni & Liveright, 1926. *New Directions, 1950.* 8 p. 1., 3-231 p.
front., plates. *"This book is for Mary Moore of Trenton, if she wants
it."* 27-1691. Copyright A 963232,
WHICH WAS RETITLED
PS3531.082P4/1971
Personae; the collected shorter poems of Ezra Pound. New York,
New Directions Pub. Corp., 1971. 281 p. illus. (A New Directions
book.) $6.50.
*Also published in London in 1952 under this title by Faber & Faber,
who republished and retitled it in 1968 as "Collected Shorter Poems,"
for which British readers can be grateful.* **811'.5'2.** 72-200880.
MARC.

PS3531.082P525/1972 Rare Book Coll.
Plaint, by Ezra Pound. *Four short poems: "350 numbered copies of
(this) keepsake were printed by Mark Holmes Walpole, Class of '74, at
the Alexander Hamilton Press, Hamilton College, Clinton, N.Y.
[Pound's Alma Mater] during the Spring of 1972." Hence the first half
of this bibliography's title.*

PS3531.082P55/1921
Poems 1918-21, including three portraits and four cantos, by Ezra
Pound. New York, Boni and Liveright, 1921. 4 p. 1., 11-90 p.
Copyright A 630824. 21-22337.

PN511.P633/1966
Polite essays by Ezra Pound. Freeport, N.Y., Books for Libraries
Press, 1966. vii, 207 p. (Essay index reprint series.) Reprint of the
1937 ed. *London, Faber and Faber, Norfolk, Conn.: New Directions,
1940.*
CONTENTS. Harold Monro. Mr. Housman at Little Bethel.
Hell. We have no battles. The prose tradition in verse. Dr.
Williams' position. James Joyce et Pécuchet. Mr. Eliot's solid merit.
'Abject and utter farce.' The teacher's mission. A letter from Dr.
Rouse to E.P. Retrospect: interlude. Prefatio aut cimiclum
tumulus. Active anthology. How to read. Civilization. Note on
Dante. **814'.5'2.** 67-22111.

PS3531.082Z533
Pound/Joyce; the letters of Ezra Pound to James Joyce, with
Pound's essays on Joyce. Edited and with commentary by Forrest
Read. New York, New Directions Pub. Corp., 1967. vi, 314 p. (A
New Directions book.) *Reissued in 1971 as New Directions paperback
NDP296, $2.75. Published in London, Faber & Faber, 1968.*
816'.5'2. 66-27616.

PS3531.082P7/1910
Provença; poems selected from Personae, Exultations, and Can-
zoniere of Ezra Pound. Boston, Small, Maynard and company,
1910. vi, 84 p. $1.00. *First American edition of Pound's works.*
10-30745 Revised, Copyright A 278142.

PS3531.082Q5 Rare Bk. Coll.
Quia pauper amavi by Ezra Pound. London, The Egoist ltd., 1919,
51.
"The edition on hand-made paper is limited to one hundred
copies, of which this is no. 55." CONTENTS: Langue d'oc.
Moeurs contemporaines. Three cantos. Homage to Sextus Propertius. *In English.* 44-46933.

PS3531.082G8/1908
A quinzaine for this Yule, being selected from a Venetian sketchbook, "San Trovaso," by Ezra Pound. London, Pollock & co., 1908. 27, 1. p. Poems. 10-6569 Revised.

PS3531.082R4 Rare Bk. Coll.
Redondillas; or, Something of that sort, by Ezra Pound. New York, New Directions, 1967. 21 p. 110 copies signed by the author. *A hitherto unpublished long poem of 1910-11 with "A Note on Pound's Redondillas" by Noel Stock.* 68-953.

PS3531.082R5 Rare Bk. Coll.
Ripostes of Ezra Pound, whereto are appended the complete poetical works of T.E. Hulme, with prefatory note. London, S. Swift and co., ltd. 1912. 63, 1 p. 44-48966.

Selected Cantos (1967 and 1970 paperbacks; see Cantos/Chronologically)

Selected Letters, 1907-1941 (1971 paperback; see Letters, 1907-1941)

PS3531.082A6/1928 Rare Bk. Coll.
Selected poems, edited with an introduction by T.S. Eliot, London, Faber & Gwyer, 1928. 2 p. 1., vii-xxxii, 184 p. Bibliography: p. xxvi. *Later reprinted in new edition 1935 and in postwar British hard- and soft-cover editions with a 1948 postscript by Eliot.*
CONTENTS: Personae of Ezra Pound (1908-10). Ripostes (1912). Lustra. Cathay. Poems from Lustra (1915). Hugh Selwyn Mauberley (Life and contacts). Early poems rejected by the author and omitted from his collected edition. 29-10931.

PS3531.082A6/1949
Selected poems. New York, New Directions, 1949. viii, 184 p. (The New classics series.) *Drawing of Ezra Pound by Wyndham* Lewis. **811.5.** 49-11526.

PS3531.082A6/1957
Selected poems. A new ed. New York, J. Laughlin, 1957. 184 p. (A New Directions paperbook, no. 66.) *All three "Selected Poems" are largely similar.* **811.5.** 57-8603.

PS3531.082A6/1940 Rare Bk. Coll.
A selection of poems, by Ezra Pound. London, Faber and Faber, 1940. 80 p. Sesame books. "Select bibliography": p. 7. **811.5.** A 41-1411.

PS3531.082A6/1973
Selected prose, 1909-1965 by Ezra Pound. Edited with an introd. by William Cookson. [New York, New Directions Pub. Corp., c1973.] 475 p. (New Directions books) $15.00. ISBN 0-8112-0465-0. *Also published in London by Faber & Faber, 1973.* 72-93978.

HG355.P68
Social credit: an impact, by Ezra Pound. London, S. Nott, 1935. 81 p. (Pamphlets on the new economics, no. 8.) *Reprinted as "Money Pamphlet" no. 5 in British series issued by Peter Russell, 1951. 20 pp., 21 = cm. paperbound. 2/6. 79-205495.*

PN681.P6 1910 Rare Bk. Coll.
The spirit of romance; an attempt to define somewhat the charm of the pre-renaissance literature of Latin Europe, by Ezra Pound. London, J.M. Dent & Sons, ltd., 1910. x, 251, 1. p. *Later, in S.S.: A New Directions book, printed in the Republic of Ireland, 1952, and subsequently in paperback as NDP 266, $2.45.*
CONTENTS. The phantom dawn. Il miglior fabbro (Arnaut Daniel.) Provenca. Geste and romance. La dolce lingua toscana. Il maestro (Dante). Montcorbier, alias Villon. The quality of Lope de Vega. Camoens. Poeti latini. 13-8344.

PS3531.082U5/1920 Rare Bk. Coll.
Umbra: the early poems of Ezra Pound, all that he now wishes to keep in circulation from "Personae," "Exultations," "Ripostes," etc. With translations from Guido Cavalcanti and Arnaut Daniel and poems by the late T. E. Hulme. London, E. Mathews, 1920. 128 p.
"One hundred copies of this edition have been printed, numbered and signed by that author, of which this is no. 30." 21-10206.

Venison, Alfred: see "Alfred Venison's Poems"

B. CONTRIBUTIONS, EDITING, TRANSLATIONS by POUND, EZRA LOOMIS, 1885-1972

tr. – translator
ed. – editor
cor. – contributor, compiler, or collaborator
(Alphabetically, by names)

PQ4299.C2/1966 Rare Bk. Coll.
Cavalcanti, Guido, d. 1300   *tr.*
Ezra Pound's Cavalcanti poems. New York, 1966. 105 p. (A New Directions book.)
"The edition consists of 190 copies on Pescia paper . . . All copies are signed by the author." This copy not signed, not numbered.
Includes Introduction to edition of 1912, Mediaevalism, and The Other Dimension, by E. Pound. *Foreword by Pound dated "Venezia, 1965." Printed in Italy.* 66-6087.

PQ4299.C2/1912 Rare Bk. Coll.
Cavalcanti, Guido, d. 1300   *tr.*
The sonnets and ballate of Guido Cavalcanti; with translation and introduction by Ezra Pound. Boston, Small, Maynard and company, 1912; *also London, S. Swift and Co., ltd., 1912.* xxiv, 119 p. $2.00. Text in Italian and English. *Dedication: "As much of this book as is mine I send to my friends VIOLET and FORD MADOX HUEFFER" (later Ford Madox Ford.)* 12-14084. Copyright A 314283.

PL2997.L82/1937 Rare Bk. Coll.
Confucius, c. 551-479 (?) B.C.   *tr.*
Digest of the Analects. Milan, P. Vera, 1937. 20 p. 1 1. Half-title: Digest of the Analects, that is, of the Philosophic conversations. On cover: Kung Fu Tseu. 896.18 40-7754.

PL2472.M6   *ed. and tr.*
Confucius: the great digest & Unwobbling pivot. Stone text from rubbings supplied by William Hawley; a note on the stone editions, by Achilles Fang. New York, 1951. 187 p. illus. "A New Directions book."
"An edition for WALTER de RACHEWILTZ" (Pound's grandson). 181.1. 51-8850 rev.

AP2.P533 no. 4   *ed. and tr.*
Confucius: the unwobbling pivot & the Great digest; translated by
Ezra Pound, with notes and commentary on the text and the
ideograms, together with Ciu Hsi's "Preface" to the Chung yung
and Tseng's commentary on the Testament. (n. p.). 1947. 52 p.
(Pharos no. 4.) 181.1. 51-20272 rev.

PL2478.F6/1959   *tr.*
"Shih ching." The Confucian odes, the classic anthology defined by
Confucius. Translation by Ezra Pound. New York, J. Laughlin,
1959. xv, 223 p. (A New Directions paperbook, NDP 81, $2.45.)
    Published in 1954 under title: The classic anthology defined by
Confucius. *Cambridge, Mass. Harvard University Press.* **895.11082.**
59-13170. (British edition by Faber, 1974).

PL2478/M6/1975   *tr.*
Ta-hsueh. Ta hio, the great learning, newly rendered into the
American language, by Ezra Pound. Seattle, University of
Washington bookstore, 1928. 35 p. 1. (*Half-title:* University of
Washington chapbooks, ed. by G. Hughes. no. 14.) "The Confucian classics are customarily divided into Five ching and the Four
shu. The first of the four shu (or books) is the Ta hio, a work of
which the first chapter is ascribed to Confucius, and the Remainder
to one of his disciples, Thseng-tseu (Tsang Tzu). – Note. 28-12445
Revised. Provisional. **181.1.** Copyright A 1074133. Reissued thrice
in Pennsylvania: Folcroft Library Editions, 1975; Norwood Editions, 1977, and Philadelphia, R. West, 1978.

PS3509.L43W3/1971
Eliot, Thomas Stearns, 1888-1965   *ed.*
The Waste Land; a facsimile transcript of the original drafts in-
cluding the annotations of Ezra Pound. Ed. by Valerie Eliot. N.Y.
Harcourt Brace Jovanovich, 1971. xxx, 149 p. facsims. 29 cm.
$22.50. **821.** ISBN 0-15-194760-0. LC 70-160401.

PL782.E5F4/1971   *ed*
Fenollosa, Ernest Francisco, 1853-1908, tr.
Certain noble plays of Japan: from the manuscripts of Ernest
Fenollosa, chosen and finished by Ezra Pound, with an introd. by
William Butler Yeats. Churchtown, Ire. Cuala Press, 1916. Shan-
non, Irish University Press, 1971. xviii, 48 p.

CONTENTS: Nishikigi, a play in two acts by Motoklyo. Hagoromo, a play in one act. Kumasaka, a play in two acts, by Ujinobu. Kagekiyo, a play in one act, by Motokiyo. **895.6'2'008.** ISBN 0-7165-1350-1. 73-25531. MARC.

PN1055.F4/1935,1936b, etc. *ed. and tr.*
Fenollosa, Ernest Francisco, 1853-1908. The Chinese written character as a medium for poetry. With offset of the Calcutta ed. of the Pivot. Washington Square $ Series (1935?). *Later reprints (San Francisco) City Lights Books.* 96 p. illus. (Square dollar series, 1.)
    Cover title. Each part has special t.p.
    CONTENTS. The unwobbling pivot & The great digest, by Confucius; translated by E. Pound. The Chinese written character as a medium for poetry, an ars poetica, by E. Fenollosa, with a foreword and notes by E. Pound. 62-57281.

PL887.F45/1950 *cor.*
Fenollosa, Ernest Francisco, 1853-1908.
The classic Noh theatre of Japan, by Ezra Pound and Ernest Fenollosa. New York, New Directions, 1959. 163 p. (A New Directions paperbook, 79). Westport CT, Greenwood Press, 1977. First published in 1916 under title: "Noh"; or, Accomplishment, a study of the classical stage of Japan, by Ernest Fenollosa and Ezra Pound. **895.62082.** 59-9488.

Fenollosa: Also SEE Part A ("By Ezra Pound") "Instigations of Ezra Pound, together with an essay on the Chinese character by Ernest Fenollosa."

QP251.G66/1932a/Delta *tr.*
Gourmont, Remy de, 1858-1915.
The natural philosophy of love, by Remy de Gourmont; translated with a postscript by Ezra Pound; introduction by Burton Rascoe; decorations by G.T. Hartmann. New York, Liveright Inc., 1932. xx, 1, 317 p. (The black and gold library). Illustrated lining papers; title vignette; head-pieces. Bibliography: p. 315-317.
    A translation of Physique de l'amour made in Paris in the early 1920's. In his postscript, Pound asserts his own opinion that man is really "the phallus or spermatozoide charging, head-on, the female chaos . . . . Even oneself has felt it, driving any new ideas into the great passive vulva of London, a sensation analogous to the male feeling in copulation." **612.6.** 32-12841.

PS3515.E37 I5/Rare Bk. Coll.   *ed.*
Hemingway, Ernest, 1899-1961.
In our time, by Ernest Hemingway, Paris, printed at the Three
Mountains Press and for sale at Shakespeare & Company; London,
W. Jackson, 1924. 3 p. 1. 9-30 p. 1 1. incl. front. (port.)
Colophon: Here ends The inquest into the state of contemporary
English prose, as edited by Ezra Pound and printed at the Three
Mountain Press. "Of 170 copies printed on rives hand-made paper
this is number 53." Subsequently printed as chapter headings in a
collection of stories by Hemingway published under the same title.
cf.Cohn, L.H. A bibliography of the works of Ernest Hemingway.
45-47635 rev.

PL2658.E3H6
Holbrook, David   *cor. and tr.*
Plucking the rushes: an anthology of Chinese poetry in translations,
by Arthur Waley, Ezra Pound and Helen Waddell; compiled by
David Holbrook. London, Heinemann Educational, 1968. ix, 118
p. 10/6. SBN 435-14440-5. (B 68-11503). **895.1'1'008.** 68-141585.

PR4826.J5/1915/Rare Bk. Coll.
Johnson, Lionel Pigot, 1867-1902   *ed*
Poetical works of Lionel Johnson. London, E. Mathews, 1915. xix
p. 1 1. 320 p. pl., 2 port. (incl. front.) Pref. signed: Ezra Pound.
15-27629.

PQ4835.E22M63/Rare Bk. Coll.
Pea, Enrick, 1881-1952.   *tr.*
Moscardinao. Translated by Ezra Pound *into Italian*. Milano,
All'Inseqna del pesce d'oro, 1956-1955. 58-33841.

HC305.P65/Rare Bk. Coll.
Por, Odon, 1883-deceased.   *tr.*
Italy's policy of social economics, 1939-1940, by Odon Por,
translated by Ezra Pound. Bergamo, Italy, etc. Instituto italiano
d'arti grafiche, 1941. 204 p. 2 1. **330.945.** 44-20466.

★   ★   ★

PS614.P78/1933/Rare Bk. Coll.
Pound, Ezra Loomis, 1885-1972   *ed.*
Active anthology, edited by Ezra Pound. London, Faber and Faber,

ltd., 1933. 255 p. ". . . writers . . . in whose verse a development appears or . . . 'still appears' to be taking place . . ." p. 5.
CONTENTS. William Carlos Williams. Basil Bunting. Louis Zukofsky. Louis Aragon, tr. by E.E. Cummings. E.E. Cummings. E. Hemingway. Marianne Moore. George Oppen. D.G. Bridson. T.S. Eliot. Ezra Pound. Notes. **811.50822.** 34-12570.

An Angle; Cantos XVII and LXXVI in facsimile of Ezra Pound's handwriting with seven stunning original lithographs by Venetian artist Giuseppe Santomaso in a handsome limited edition published spring 1972 by Erker-Presse, Gallusstrasse 32, CH-9000 St. Gallen, Switzerland. Only 200 copies (each accompanied by a recording of Pound reading his text) with proceeds to UNESCO'S International Campaign to Save Venice.
NOTE: The same publisher has also issued, in 1973, an anthology, Erker-Treffen, containing seven handwritten words by Pound. Set off with a work of art by Max Bill.

PL3277.EP6/Rare Bk. Coll.   *tr.*
Cathay; translations by Ezra Pound, for the most part from the Chinese of Rihaku, from the notes of the late Ernest Fenollosa, and the decipherings of the professors Mori and Ariga. London, E. Mathews, 1915. 31, 1.p.
Rihaku is the Japanese form of the name of the Chinese poet, Li Po or Li T'ai-po. "The seafarer (from the early Anglo-Saxon text)": p. 23-27. 15-15688. PL2969 P6.

PJ1945.P59   *tr. and cor.*
Come swiftly to your love; love poems of ancient Egypt. Translated by Ezra Pound and Noel Stock. Illustrated by Tom di Grazia. Kansas City, Mo., Hallmark Cards, Inc., c 1971. *Hence the second half of this bibliography's title.* 44 p. illus. (Hallmark editions.) $2.50.
"Based on literal renderings of the hieroglyphic texts into Italian by *Pound's son-in-law* Boris de Rachewiltz, which first appeared in the volume Lirichie amorose degli antichi egizioni (sic) published . . . in 1957."
1962 ed. published under title: Love poems of ancient Egypt. **801'.3.** 74-127744. MARC. ISBN 0-87529-175-9.

PL2472.R6 *ed. and tr.*
(Chinese into Italian)
Confucio: studio integrale & L'asse che non vacilla. Verzione e commento di Ezra Pound, con una nota sui classici in pietra di Achilles Fang. Milano, All'insegna del pesce d'oro, 1955. 105 p. (*His* Scritti italiani.) Chinese and Italian.
"Studi e traduzioni di E.P. dal cinese e giapponese": 194-195. 62-25863.

PN6014.P645/1964 *ed., tr., and cor.*
Confucius to Cummings, an anthology of poetry. Edited by Ezra Pound and Marcella Spann. New York, New Directions Pub. Corp., 1964. xxii, 353 p. (A New Directions book.) *Also available in New Directions paperback NDP 126, $2.95.* **808.81.** 62-17274.

ed.
The Exile; edited and published by Ezra Pound. no. 1-4; spring 1927-autumn 1928. Dijon, M. Darantiere; etc., etc., 1927-28. 92, 3, 121, 3, 109, 3, 117 p. 2 no. a year. No 1 has imprint on cover: Dijon, M. Darantiere; no. 2-3. Chicago, P. Covici; no.4, New York, Covici Friede. *Shortlived quarterly review. First issue was printed in Europe, but delayed at U.S. Customs because "the fellow that wrote that stuff . . . must be a dope fiend. Nobody has thoughts like that except under the influence of drugs."* 29-29190. AP2. E963.

PJ1945.P6 *tr. and cor.*
Love poems of Ancient Egypt, translated by E. Pound and Noel Stock. Norfolk, Conn. New Directions, 1962. 33 p. illus. *(Paperback NDP 178, $1.50)*
"Based on literal renderings of the hieroglyphic texts innto Italian by Boris de Rachewiltz, which first appeared in the volume Liriche ambroso degli antichi egizioni (sic) published . . . in 1957."
1971 ed. published under title: Come swiftly to your love. *Kansas City, Mo. Hallmark Cards.* **893.11082.** 62-16925.

PJ1945.P612/Orien Arab
"Love Poems of ancient Egypt" also available in Arabic edition. Library of Congress catalog no. 79-961672.

PR1225.P6/Office   *cor.*
Profile; an anthology collected in MCMXXXI. Milan. Tipograffia
Card. Ferrari, 1932. 3 p. 1., 9-142 p., 3 l.
At head of title: Ezra Pound. "Edition privately printed for John
Scheiwiller limited to 250 numbered copies. Copy n. 47."
"Merely the poems that I happen to remember", with comments.
p. 13. **821.910822.** 33-7944.

PR1772.A34/Rare Bk. Coll.   *tr.*
The Seafarer. From the Anglo-Saxon. With a portrait of the poet by
Oskar Kokoschka. Frankfurt am Main, Ars librorum (1965). xiii p.
(Ars librorum Druck, II.) DM 260.- (GDNB 66-A26-200.)
"The Seafarer" is taken from "Personae" of Ezra Pound, Faber
and Faber of London; New Directions, New York. 66-69946.

PN6020.P6/1963   *tr.*
Translations. With an introd. by Hugh Kenner. Enl. ed. Norfolk,
Conn. New Directions, 1963. 448 p. (A New Directions paperbook,
145). $2.95. Westport, CT, Greenwood Press, 1978.
Includes some original poems, with translations on opposite
pages. First published in 1954 under title: The translations of Ezra
Pound. *London: Faber paper-covered editions, 1970, £1.25.* **808.8.**
64-1552.

                            ★   ★   ★

PA4414.T7P6   *tr.*
Sophocles, c. 496-406 *B.C.*
Women of Trachis, a version by Ezra Pound. New York, New
Directions, 1957. xxiii, 66 p. port. A play.
London: Faber paper covered edition, 1969. **882.2.** 56-6530.

PR6047.E3Z55/1917   *ed.*
Yeats, John Butler, 1839-1922.
Passages from the letters of John Butler Yeats: selected by Ezra
Pound. Churchtown, Dundrum, The Cuala press, 1917. 4 p. 1., 60
p., 1 l.
Colophon: Here ends 'Passages from the letters of John Butler
Yeats . . . Published and printed by Elizabeth Corbet Yeats. 400
copies.

John Butler Yeats, painter, was father of William Butler Yeats. 17-23318.

C. ABOUT POUND, EZRA LOOMIS, 1885-1972

(Alphabetically, mostly by author)

PS3531.O82/Z5365/1980
Ackroyd, Peter
Ezra Pound and his world. New York, Scribner, 1980. 127 p., illus., ports., index, bib. ISBN: 0-684-16798-0. 811'.52B19 80-5795.

PS3531.O82/C292/1975
Adams, John (1753-1826) and Sanders, Frederick K.
John Adams speaking: Pound's sources for the Adams Cantos. Orono, University of Maine Press, 1975? 530 p. **811'.5'2.** 75-620003

PS3531.O82Z538/Rare Bk. Coll.
Aldington, Richard, 1892-
Ezra Pound and T.S. Eliot; a lecture. Hurst, Berks. Peacocks Press, 1954. 20 p. In case.
"Three hundred and fifty copies printed in Baskerville on Barcham Green 'Medway' paper." **811.5** 55-16324.

PS3531.O82Z539
Alexander, Michael J.
The poetic achievement of Ezra Pound. Berkeley, University of California Press, 1979. 247 p. **811'.5'2.** 78-59449

PS3531.O82Z54/1966
Amdur, Alice Steiner
The poetry of Ezra Pound. New York, Russell & Russell, 1966. 106 p. First published in 1936. Bib. p. 103-6. **811.52.** 66-13161.

ML410.A638A3
Antheil, George, 1900-1959
Bad boy of music, Garden City, N.Y., Doubleday, Doran and Co., inc., 1945. vi, 378 p.
Autobiography, "First edition" *in which the composer bites that hand that pushed him forth.* **920[B].**

PS3531.O82Z544
Bacigalupo, Massimo, 1947-
   The formed trace: the later poetry of Ezra Pound, New York, Columbia University Press, 1980. 512 p. **811'.5'2.** 79-12877

PS3515.E37Z575/1969
Baker, Carlos Heard, 1909-
   Ernest Hemingway; a life story. N.Y. Scribner, 1969. xvi, 697 p. 2 illus. ports. *Bantam Paperback Y5554, $1.95, 1970. In which Pound is a more-than-incidental character.* **813'.5'2 [B]**. 68-57074. MARC.

Bauman, Walter
   The Rose in the Steel Dust: An Examination of the Cantos of Ezra Pound. Coral Gables, Fla.: University of Miami Press, 1973. 211 p., $5.95.
   The author is Lecturer in German at Magee University College, Londonderry, Northern Ireland. **811.** 73-102691.

Z305.B32
Beach, Sylvia
   Shakespeare and Company, 1st. ed., New York, Harcourt, Brace, 1959. 230 p. illus. *Portraits of Pound, pp. 26-27. Subtitled "The Story of an American Bookshop in Paris" in Harvest Books (Harcourt, Brace) paperback HB97, $1.65, but without illustrations. By the owner, who also published Joyce's* Ulysses *in 1922. Some great vignettes of Pound.* **818.**

PS3531.O82C2836
Bernstein, Michael Andre, 1947-
   The tale of the tribe: Ezra Pound and the modern verse epic. Princeton, NJ, Princeton University Press, 1980. 320 p. Hardcover and paperback. **811'.0309.** 80-129

PS3531.O82Z547
Bornstein, George
   The postromantic consciousness of Ezra Pound. Victoria, B.C. (Canada), English Literary Studies, University of Victoria, 1977. 84 p. **811'.5'2.** 78-308986

PS3531.O82Z55
Brooke-Rose, Christine, 1923-
A ZBC of Ezra Pound. 1st ed., London, Faber and Faber, 1971.
x, 297 p. £2.75. Bibliography: p. 272-280. 811',5'2. 70-888171.
MARC ISBN 0-571-09135-0.

PS3531.082C2927
Brooke-Rose, Christine, 1923-
A structural analysis of Pound's Usura canto. The Hague
(Netherlands), Mouton, 1976. 76 p. **811'.5'4.** 76-377402

PS3531.082Z5513
Brooker, Peter
A student's guide to the selected poems of Ezra Pound. London &
Boston, Faber & Faber, 1979. 367 p. **811'.5'2.** 79-670305

Z733.U63B65
The Case against the Saturday review of literature; the attack of
the Saturday review on modern poets and critics, answered by the
Fellows of American Letters of the Library of Congress, together
with articles, editorials and letters from other writers. Chicago,
Poetry, 1949. vi. 71 p. 811.5079' 50-50.

PS3531.082/C293
Bush, Ronald
The genesis of Ezra Pound's Cantos. Princeton, NJ, Princeton
University Press, 1976. 327 p. **811'.5'2.** 76-3245

PS3531.082/Z553
Chace, William M.
The Political Identities of Ezra Pound and T.S. Eliot. Stanford,
CA., Stanford University Press, 1973. ISBN 0-8047-0843-6.
821'.9'1209 73-80620

PS3531.082/E96/1978
Contino, Vittorugo
Ezra Pound in Italy. From the Pisan cantos. Spots & dots.
Venezia, G. Ivancich, 1970. 75, 1. illus. It 70-July. Library's text in
Italian; excerpts from the cantos in English and Italian. New York,
Rizzoli, 1978. **811'.5'2.** 77-95288

KF224.P6C6
Cornell, Julien, D., 1910-
The trial of Ezra Pound: a documented account of the treason case by the defendant's lawyer, Julien Cornell. *New York, John Day Co., 1966. London, Faber, 1967.* 216 p. facsims. (B 67-17873). "Appendix iv. Transcript of trial; transcript of hearing in the United States District Court for the District of Columbia, February 13, 1946": p. 154-215. 843.3'1. 68-71008.

A narrative collection of letters, documents, and transcripts – among which are some unique quotes and handwritten samples from Pound. But it is self-serving, in a well-meaning way, in that it makes a one-sided case for insanity as Pound's defense. Cornell does bend over backwards not to sound bitter about his replacement as counsel by Thurman Arnold in the final proceedings that obtained Pound's release.

PS221.C65/1951
Cowley, Malcolm, 1898.
Exile's return; a literary odyssey of the 1920s. New ed. New York, Viking Press, 1956. vi, 322 p.

Viking Compass Paperback, C4, 1956, $2.25. 14th printing, June 1972; Pound glimpsed in passing by a perceptive outsider, in this updating of a 1934 classic which didn't have much about him. **810.9.**

PS310.P6C7/1981
Craig, Cairns
Yeats, Eliot, Pound, and the politics of poetry: riches to the richest. Pittsburgh, University of Pittsburgh Press, 1982. 323 p., index, bib. **821'.912'09358** 19 81-11607

PS3505.U334Z53
Cummings, Edward Estlin, 1894-1962.
Selected letters of E.E. Cummings. Ed. by F.W. Dupee and George Stade. 1st ed. N.Y. Harcourt, Brace & World, 1969. xxiv, 296 p. illus. ports. *"Letters of E.E. Cummings to Ezra Pound" were also published in* Paris Review. *vol. 10, pp. 55-87. Fall 1966.* **811.**

PS221.C8/1969
Curley, Dorothy Nyren, *comp.*
Modern American Literature. Compiled and edited by Dorothy Nyren Curley, Maurice Kramer and Ealine Fialka Kramer. 4th enl. ed. New York, Frederick Ungar Pub. Co. 3v. 472 $ 490 $ 515 pp. (A

library of literary criticisms.) Includes bibliographies. $45.00. *Excellent section on Pound, Vol. III, pp. 23-32.* SBN 8044-3046-2. **810.9'005.**

PS3554/A86G4/1981
Davenport, Guy
   The geography of the imagination: 40 essays. Berkeley, CA, North Point Press, 1981. 384 p., incl. bibliog. refs., **814'.54.** 80-23870.
   Critical writings exalting Pound as the greatest modern aesthetic intelligence.

PS3531.082Z58
Davie, Donald
   Ezra Pound: poet as sculptor. New York, Oxford University Press, 1964. viii, 261 p. port. Bibliographical footnotes. *Oxford Univ. Press Galaxy paperback.* GB 2470, 1968. $1.75.
   Solid critical study of Pound's literary art. **811.52.** 64-24860.

PS3531.082Z582
Davie, Donald
   Ezra Pound. Part of the Modern Masters series edited by Frank Kermode. New York, Viking Press and Penguin Books 1976. (British edition published London, Fontana, 1975, under title "Pound") 134 p. **811'.5'2.** 76-112, 76-27980, and 75-331216

PS3531.082Z59
Davis, Earle Rosco, 1905-
   Vision fugitive; Ezra Pound and economics, by Earle Davis. Lawrence, University Press of Kansas, 1968. xiv, 213 p. $6.95. Bib references included in "Notes" (p. 203-208). **811'.5'2.** 68-25819.

PS3531.082C284/1963
Dekker, George
   The cantos of Ezra Pound; a critical study. New York, Barnes & Noble, 1963. xvi, 207 p. First published in 1963 in England (London, Routledge & Kegan Paul) under title: Sailing after knowledge. Bibliographical footnotes. **811.52.** 63-23827.

PL2478.F63D4
Dembo, L.S.
The Confucian odes of Ezra Pound; a critical appraisal. Berkeley
University of California Press, 1963. 111 p. (Perspectives in
criticism, 12.) 895.11082. 63-12817.

PS3531.082C259/1981
Dilligan, Robert J.; Parins, James W. and Bender, Todd K.
A concordance to Ezra Pound's Cantos. New York, Garland,
1981. 612 p. **811'.52**. 77-83375.

PS3531.082Z595/1979
Doolittle, Hilda, 1886-1961
End to torment: a memoir of Ezra Pound by "H.D." Edited by
Norman Holmes Pearson and Michael King, with the poems from
"Hilda's book by Ezra Pound." New York, New Directions 1979.
84 p.m **811'.5'2**. 78-27149

Z8709.3.E3/1974
Edwards, John Hamilton, 1922-
A preliminary checklist of the writings of Ezra Pound, especially
his contributions to periodicals. With an introd. by Norman
Holmes Pearson. New Haven, Kirgo-Books, 1953. viii, 73 p. *Good
bibliographic reference source by editor of "The Pound Newsletter."*
012. 52-12855 rev. Folcroft, PA, Folcroft Library Editions, 1974.
74-22321. Norwood, PA. Norwood Editions, 1977. 77-25431

PS3531.082Z6
Eliot, Thomas Stearns, 1888-1964
Ezra Pound, his metric and poetry. New York, A.A. Knopf,
1917. 31 p. front. "Bibliography of books and partial bibliography
of notable critical articles by Ezra Pound": p. 29-31. 811.5.
18-17475 rev.

PR5906.E38
Ellmann, Richard, 1918-
Eminent Domain; Yeats among Wilde, Joyce, Pound, Eliot and
Auden. New York, Oxford University Press, 1967. **821.** 67-25458

PS3531.082C285
Emery, Clark Mixon, 1909-
Ideas into action; a study of Pound's Cantos. Coral Gables, Fla.,

University of Miami Press, 1958. xi, 196 p. (University of Miami publications in English and American literature, no. 111.) Erratum slip inserted. Bibliography: p. 183-187. *Forward by Norman Holmes Pearson, Yale Univ.* 811.52. 58-14060.

PS3531.082H842/1955
Espey, John Jenkins, 1913-
  Ezra Pound's Mauberley; a study in composition. Berkeley, University of California Press, 1955. London, Faber & Faber, 1955. 139 p. 811.5. 54-6474.

PS3531.082Z624
Ezra Pound Conference, 1st
  Held at Sheffield University, Sheffield England. New York, AMS Press, 1978. 166 p. 77-78316

Z8709.3.F3 Rare Bk. Coll.
Farmer, David
  Ezra Pound: an exhibition held in March 1967, the Academic Center and Undergraduate Library, the University of Texas. Austin, 1967. 62 p. illus. facsims. ports. *(Bibliography and catalog)* "Published on the occasion of a symposium entitled: Make it new: translation and metrical innovations, aspects of Ezra Pound's work, the University of Texas, March 15-17, 1967." "Acknowledgments" by the Humanities Research Center, University of Texas. 016.818'.5'209. 67-64638.

PR9199.3.F52F3/1982
Findley, Timothy
  Famous Last Words. A novel in which Pound's Hugh Selwyn Mauberley dances with the Duchess of Windsor. New York, Delacorte Press/Seymour Lawrence, 1982. 396 p. ISBN 0-440-02477-3. **813'.54 19** 82-1430

PS3531.082/C2935
Flory, Wendy Stallard
  Ezra Pound and the Cantos: a record of struggle. New Haven, Yale University Press, 1980. 321 p. illus. **811'.5'2.** 79-23904

PS3531.082Z63/1965
Fraser, George Sutherland, 1915-
  Ezra Pound by G.S. Fraser. New York, Barnes & Noble, 1965,

1960. 118 p. (Writers and critics.) Bibliography: p. 115-118.
811.52. 65-8598.

T14.5/F94
Fuller, Richard Buckminster
Pound, synergy, and the great design: third Pound lecture on the
humanities. Moscow, University of Idaho, 1977. 21 p., illus.
301.24'3. 78-621620

PS3531.082Z633
Furbank, Philip Nicholas
Ezra Pound, prepared for a third-level arts course on 20th cen-
tury poetry and published in England by Milton Keynes, Open
University Press, 1975. 52 p., facsims., ports. **811'.5'2.** 76-378169

Z8709.3.G3
Gallup, Donald Clifford, 1913-
A bibliography of Ezra Pound by Donald Gallup. London, Hart-
Davis, 1963. 454 p. facsims., port. (Soho bibs., 18.) *The best
bibliography updated periodically in* Paideuma *(see end of this
sections).* **016.81152.** 64-3947.

Z8709.3.G32 Rare Bk. Coll.
Gallup, Donald Clifford, 1913-
On contemporary bibliography, with particular reference to Ezra
Pound by Donald Gallup. Austin Humanities Research Center,
University of Texas, 1970. 28 p. front. (Bibliographical monograph
series, no. 4.) "Printed in an edition of 500 copies." **010'.28**
73-630258. MARC.

PS3509.L43Z6747
Gallup, Donald Clifford, 1913-
T.S. Eliot & Ezra Pound, collaborators in letters, by Donald
Gallup. 1st ed. New Haven, Conn. H.W. Wenning/C.A. Stonehill,
1970. 50 p. "This article is reprinted with a few slight revisions
from the Atlantic monthly for January, 1970." Includes
bibliographical references. **821'.9'1209.** 74-20850. MARC.

PS3531.082Z635/1974
Giovannini, Giovanni, 1906-
Ezra Pound and Dante. New York, Haskell House, 1974. 18 p.
811'.5'2. 74-7249

PS3531.082Z64
Goodwin, K.L.
The influence of Ezra Pound by K.L. Goodwin. London, New
York, etc. Oxford U.P., 1966. iii-xvi, 230 p. 80/. Bib. footnotes.
On Yeats, Eliot, Cummings, Lowell, Aiken, MacLeish, William
Carlos Williams, Hart Crane, Marianne Moore, Charles Olson,
Herbert Read, Wallace, Stevens, R.S. Thomas, and Donald Bot-
trall. (B 66-24488.) **811'.5'2.** 67-75817.

Microfilm/AC-1/no. 11,285
Gross, Harvey Seymour, 1922-
The contrived corridor: a study in modern poetry and the meaning of history. Ann Arbor, University Microfilms, 1955. (University Microfilms, Ann Arbor, Mich. Publication no. 11,285.)
Microfilm copy of transcript. Positive. Collection of the original:
iii, 202 I. Thesis-University of Michigan. Abstracted in Dissertation abstracts, v. 15 (1955) no. 4, p. 583. Bibliography: leaves
198-202. Microfilm AC-1. no. 11,285. Mic A 55-747.

PS3531.082Z6412
Gugelberger, Georg M.
Ezra Pound's medievalism. European university papers, series
18, comparative literature, vol. 17. Frankfurt (W. Germany), Bern
(Switzerland), Las Vegas: Lang, 1978. 214 p. **811'.52-dc19.**
81-452270.

Hall, Donald
Ezra Pound interviewed in Paris Review. Writers at Work: 2d
Series. New York, Viking Compass Paperback, 1963, pp. 35-59.
808.
Pound: "Take the serious side of Disney, the Confucian side of
Disney. It's in having taken an ethos as he does in Perri, that squirrel
film, where you have the values of courage and tenderness asserted in a
way that everybody can understand. You have an absolute genius there.
You have got a greater correlation of nature than you have had since
the time of Alexander the Great."

PS3531.082Z6416
Harmon, William
Time in Ezra Pound's work. Chapel Hill, University of North
Carolina Press, 1977. 165 p. **811'.5'2.** 77-5958

PS3531.082Z642
Henault, Marie
The Merrill guide to Ezra Pound by Marie Henault. Columbus,
Ohio, Merrill, 1970.) 46 p. (Charles E. Merrill program in
American Literature.) 811'.5'2. 71-119841. MARC.

Z8700.3.H45
Henault, Marie
The Merrill checklist of Ezra Pound. *(Bibliography.)* Columbus,
Ohio, Merrill, 1970. iv, 44 p. (Charles E. Merrill program in
American literature.) *016.811'5'2.* 75-103887.

PS3531.082/c2855
Henault, Marie   *cor.*
The Merrill studies in The Cantos. Columbus, Ohio, C.E. Mer-
rill Pub. Co., 1971. viii, 125 p. (Charles E. Merrill program in
American literature.) Title on cover: Studies in The Cantos. In-
cludes bibliographical references. 811'.5'2. 78-168862.

PS3531.082644/1969b
Hesse, Eva   *cor.*
New approaches to Ezra Pound; a co-ordinated investigation of
Pound's poetry and ideas. Edited with an introd. by Eva Hesse.
Berkeley, University of California Press, *and London, Faber, 1969. A
book by Pound's German translator first published in Frandfurt, 1967,
under title of "Ezra Pound: 22 Versuche über einen Dichter."* 406 p.
8.50, Biblio. footnotes, 811'.5'2. 76-78928. MARC.

PS3531.082Z645
Heymann, Clemens David, 1945-
Ezra Pound, the last rower: a political profile. New York, Viking
Press, 1976. Seaver Books paperbound, 1980. 372 p., illus. 811'.5'2.
74-4803 and 80-52073.

PS2123.H6/1966
Holder, Alan, 1932-
Three voyagers in search of Europe; a study of Henry James,
Ezra Pound, and T.S. Eliot. Philadelphia, University of Penn-
sylvania Press, 1966. 396 p. Biblio.: p. 361-389. **818.409.** 64-24513.

PS3531.082/Z467
Homberger, Eric
Ezra Pound: The Critical Heritage. London and Boston: Routledge and Kegan Paul, The Critical Heritage Series, 1972. 500 p., $21.50. **811'.5'2.** 72-90114
The editor is Lecturer in American Literature at the University of East Anglia. ISBN 0-7100-7260-0.

PS3531.082Z65
Hutchins, Patricia.
Ezra Pound's Kensington; an exploration, 1885-1913. Chicago, Regnery, 1965. 180 p. illus. ports. Bibliographical references included in "Notes" (p. 161-70). **928.1.** 65-2305.

PS3531.082Z66
Italian Images of Ezra Pound: 12 critical essays edited and translated by Angelo Jung and Guido Palandri. Taipei, Mei Ya Publications, 1979. 167 p. **811'.5'2.** 79-116260.

PS3531.082Z67
Jackson, Thomas H.
The early poetry of Ezra Pound, by Thomas H. Jackson. Cambridge, Harvard University Press, 1968. ix, 261 p. illus. $6.95. Bibliographical references included in "Notes" (p. 243-255). **811'.5'2.** 68-25612.

P5310.M4J8
Juhasz, Suzanne
Metaphor and the poetry of Williams, Pound, and Stevens. Lewisburg, PA, Bucknell University Press, 1974. 292 p. **811.5'208.** 72-13393.

PS356.A4178/C3
Kaminsky, Daniel
Canto the last. *"An attempt to finish Ezra Pound's huge opus, the Cantos."* Cleveland, Pranayama Publications, 1976. 8 p. **811'.5'2.** 76-36162.

PS3531.082C294
Kearns, George
Guide to Ezra Pound's Selected Cantos. New Brunswick, NJ, Rutgers University Press, 1980. 306 p. **811'.5'2.** 80-10306.

CT775.K46
Kenin, Richard
Return to Albion: Americans in England 1760-1940, introd. by
Alistair Cooke. New York, Holt, Rinehart and Winston, 1979. 288
p. **920'.042.** 78-1033 MARC.
*From Benjamin West and Gilbert Stuart to Pound and Eliot, the
subject of a 1979 exhibit at the National Portrait Gallery in
Washington, organized by the author, an Oxford-educated American.*

PS3531.082Z7/1951a
Kenner, Hugh
The poetry of Ezra Pound. London, Faber & Faber, 1951. *New
York, New Directions.* 342 p. Bibliography: p. 334-339. *Dedicated
"To Marshall McLuhan 'A Catalogue, his jewels of conversation.'"*
811'.5'2. 52-19520.

PS3531.082Z712
Kenner, Hugh
The Pound era. Berkeley, University of California Press, 1971,
and Faber, London, 1972. xiv, 606 p. illus. $14.95. Includes
bibliographical references. *A difficult but rewarding exploration of
Pound and his contemporaries.* **811'.5'2.** 72-138349. MARC. ISBN
0-520-01800-5.

PS3531.082714
Knapp, James F.
Ezra Pound. Twayne's U.S. author series no. 348. Boston,
Twayne publishers, 1979. 177 p., port. **811'.5'2.** 79-14762.

PS3531.082Z7213
Lander, Jeannette
Ezra Pound. New York, Frederick Ungar Pub. Co., 1971. 122 p.
(Modern literature monographs.) Bibliography: p. 115-116. **B.Pou.**

PE1010.E5/1953
Leary, Lewis Gaston, 1906-   *ed.*
Motive and method in The cantos of Ezra Pound. New York, Col-
umbia University Press, 1954. vii, 135 p. (English Institute. Essays,
1953) **811'.5'2.** 54-11609.
PR3531.082C286/1969b
Reprinted 1969 by AMS Press, Inc.

PN83.P63/L4
Leavis, Frank Raymond, 1895-
  How to teach reading, a primer for Ezra Pound, by F.H. Leavis.
Cambridge, Eng., G. Fraser, The Minority Press, 1932. 3 p. 1., 49,
1 p. Occasioned by Ezra Pound's "How to read." **801'.95** Reissued
thrice in Pennsylvania: Folcroff Library edition, 1974; Norwood
Editions, 1976, and Philadelphia, R. West, 1977.
CONTENTS. Critical of Mr. Pound. Positive suggestions. 028.
33-30422.

PR601.L4/1950
Leavis, Frank Raymond, 1895-
  New bearings in English poetry; a study of the contemporary
situation. New ed. New York, G.W. Stewart, 1950. 238 p. CON-
TENTS. Prefatory note. Poetry and the modern world. The situa-
tion at the end of World War I. T.S. Eliot. Ezra Pound. Gerard
Manley Hopkins. Epilogue. Retrospect, 1950. **821.9109.** 50-10030.
New York, AMS Press, 1978. 75-30032.

PS3531.082Z734
Levin, Harry
  Ezra Pound, T.S. Eliot and the European Horizon. The Taylorian
lecture for 1974. Oxford, Clarendon Press, 1975. 27 p. **811'.5'209.**
75-317865.

AP2.C5636/No. 2,/1964
Livi, Grazia
  Interview with Ezra Pound in City Lights Journal no. 3, 1964,
pp. 37-46. San Francisco, City Lights Books. This appeared first in
Italian in *Epoca,* Milan, March 24, 1963. It was translated and pro-
mptly disclaimed by Jean McLean: "It is as though a Fleet Street
hack were sent to interview and question Buddha . . . But, as I considered the Italian text, I was haunted by thought of what a
translator less familiar than I with Pound during this period might
do to it." Despite such harrumphing, this is well worth reading. A
cover photo shows Pound walking in Venice.

PS3531.082P53/Rare Bk. Coll.
MacLeish, Archibald, 1892-1982
  Poetry and opinion; the Pisan cantos of Ezra Pound, a dialog on
the role of poetry. Urbana, University of Illinois Press, 1950. 52 p.

The argument over the prize to Pound presented in the form of a debate between a "Mr. Bollingen" and a "Mr. Saturday," symbolizing The Saturday Review of Literature. **811.5.** 50-12207. New York, Haskell House, 1974, 74-2189.

PS3531.082743
Makin, Peter
Provençe and Pound. Berkeley, University of California Press, 1978. 428 p. **811'.5'2.** 77-76186.

PS324.M37
Materer, Timothy
Vortex: Pound, Eliot and Lewis. Ithica, NY, Cornell University Press, 1979. 231 p., illus. **820'.9'00912.** 79-13009.

PS3531.082Z75/Rare Bk. Coll.
Mayfield, John S., 1904-
The black badge of treason, an account of Ezra Pound, by John S. Mayfield. Washington, D.C., Park Book Shop, 1944. 32 p. A 44-2188.

PS3525.A1143Z5/1968
McAlmon, Robert, 1896-1956.
Being geniuses together. Rev. and with supplementary chapters by Kay Boyle, 1st ed. in the USA. xiv, 392 p. illus. facsims. ports. Garden City, N.Y. Doubleday, 1968. *Paris in the twenties with personal glimpses of Pound.* **818M.**

PS3531.082Z74
McDougal, Stuart Y.
Ezra Pound and the Troubadour Tradition. Princeton, NJ; Princeton Univ. Press, 1972. 159 p., $8, **811'.5'2.** 72-2575. ISBN 0-691-06236-6.

PS3509.L43/W3689
McLuhan, Herbert Marshall
The possum and the midwife: lecture on Eliot, Pound, and "The Waste Land." Moscow, University of Idaho, 1978. 21 p., ports. **821'.912** 78-623925.

PS3731.082Z758
Meacham, Harry M.
The caged panther; Ezra Pound at Saint Elizabeth's by Harry M. Meacham. New York, Twayne Publishers, 1967. 222 p. facsims., ports. Biblio. references in "Notes" (p. 205-212) **B-Pound.** 67-30723.

PS3531.082Z754
Montgomery, Marion
Ezra Pound; a critical essay. Grand Rapids, Eerdmans, 1970. 48 p., (Contemporary writers in Christian perspective.) 0.95. Bibliography: p. 46-48. 1. Pound, Ezra Loomis, 1885- **811'.5'2.** 67-28385. MARC.

PS3531.082Z755
Mullins, Eustace Clarence, 1923-
This difficult individual, Ezra Pound. New York, Fleet Pub. Corp. 1961 288 p. illus.
A biography by a Virginia aristocrat who befriended Pound during his stay in St. Elizabeth's hospital and visited him often: with photos by the author. **928.1** 61-7628

PS3531.082Z76
Nagy, Niclas Christoph de
The poetry of Ezra Pound; the pre-imagist stage. Bern, Francke, 1960. 183 p. (The Cooper monographs in English and American language and literature, 4.) Biblio on p. 179-183. **811'.5'2.** 61-349.

PS3531.082Z757
Nänny, Max
Ezra Pound; poetics for an electric age. Bern, Francke, 1973. The McLuhanite viewpoint. 122 p., **811'.5'2.** 73-100114.

PS3531.082/C2865
Nassar, Eugene Paul
The Cantos of Ezra Pound: the lyric mode. Baltimore, Johns Hopkins University Press, 1975, 164 p. **811'.5'2.** 75-11343

AS36.W62/no. 86
Nelson, Francis William, 1922-
 The waste land manuscript. Wichita, Kan., Wichita State University, 1971. 9 p. (Kansas State University, Wichita. University studies, no. 86.) (Wichita State University, Bulletin, v. 47, no. 1) Includes biblio references. **081 s.** 79-634525. MARC.

PS3531.082Z77/1968
Norman, Charles, 1904-
 The case of Ezra Pound. New York, Funk & Wagnalls, 1968. x, 209 p. illus., ports. *Contains a comprehensive and interesting presentation of Pound's broadcasts in Italy and hearings in Washington.* **811'.5'2.** 68-16761.

PS3531.082Z773/1969b
Norman, Charles, 1904-
 Ezra Pound. Rev. ed. New York, Minerva Press, 1969. xvi, 493 p. illus., prots. $2.95. *Paperback 1956.* Biblio references included in "Notes" (p. 400-477). *London, MacDonald & Co., 1969, An important biography. (See Part 3.)* **811'.5'2.** 72-9512 MARC.

PS3531.082Z78
O'Connor, William Van, 1915-and Stone, Edward,   *eds.*
 A casebook on Ezra Pound; pro and con selections to be used as controlled source material for the freshman English course, edited by William Van O'Connor and Edward Stone. New York, Crowell, 1959. 179 p. Includes biblio.
 The very best of the casebooks about Pound's incarceration. (See Part 3.) **928.1.** 59-9400.

PS3531.082Z783/1963
O'Connor, William Van, 1915-
 Ezra Pound. Minneapolis, University of Minnesota Press, 1963. 48 p. (Minnesota. University. Pamphlets on American writers, no. 26.) Includes biblio. **811'.5'2.** 63-62712.

PS3531.082Z853/1975
Olson, Charles
 Charles Olson & Ezra Pound: an encounter at St. Elizabeth's.

Edited by Catherine Seelye. New York, Grossman, 1975. 143 p.
811'.5'2. 75-14299.

PS2531.082C287
Pearlman, Daniel D.
The barb of time; on the unity of Ezra Pound's Cantos. New York,
Oxford University Press, 1969. x, 318 p. Illus. 8.50. Biblio. foot-
notes. **811'.5'2.** 71-83015. MARC.

PS3531.082Z786
The Pound newsletter. 1-10; Jan. 1954-Apr. 1956. Berkeley, Calif.
10 no. in 1 v. quarterly. Edited by J. Edwards. *By and about Pound
while he was in St. Elizabeth's.* 64-4717.

Z8504.39P68
Pound, Omar S., and Grover, Philip
Wyndham Lewis: a descriptive bibliography. Folkestone,
Dawson, 1978. 198 p., 6 leaves of plates, illus. 78-315951.

Microfilm AC-1 no. 24,181
Pratt, William Crouch, 1927-
Revolution without betrayal: James, Pound, Eliot and the Euro-
pean tradition. Ann Arbor, University Microfilms, 1957. (Universi-
ty Microfilms, Ann Arbor, Mich. Publication no. 24,181.)
Microfilm copy (positive) of typescript. Collation of the original:
441 1. Thesis – Vanderbilt University. Abstracted in Dissertation
Abstracts, v. 17 (1957) no. 11, p. 2600. Biblio.: leaves 443-441.
Mic-4181.

PS323.5/P7
Pritchard, William H.
Lives of the modern poets. New York, Oxford University Press,
1980. 316 p. **821'.9'12.** 79-17615 MARC.

PS3531.082Z788
Quinn, Sister Mary Bernetta
Ezra Pound: an introduction to the viewpoint. New York, Columbia University Press, 1972. xiv, 191 p. (Columbia introductions to
twentieth-century American poetry. $8.95. Biblio: p. 179-184.
*"Written for the nonspecialist, but with new insights and facts not ap-
pearing elsewhere."* ISBN 0-231-03282. **821.** 72-6830.

131

PS3531.082Z79
Rachewiltz, Mary de
Discretions. 1st ed. Boston, Little, Brown, 1971. 312 p. illus. ports. $8.95. Includes biblio reference. *His Daughter's Book. Also published in London by Faber & Faber, 1971, and later in paperback by New Directions, retitled Ezra Pound, Father and Teacher: Discretions.* **811'.5'2.** 73-143717. MARC. 76-352215.

PS3531.082C296
Read, Forrest
One world and the Cantos of Ezra Pound. Chapel Hill, University of North Carolina Press, 1981. 476 p., illus. **811'.5'2.** 80-15892.

PS3531.082Z792
Reck, Michael
Ezra Pound; a close-up. 1st ed. New York, McGraw-Hill, 1967. xi, 205 p. **811'5'2.** 67-22962.

PS3507.0726Z85
Robinson, Janice Stevenson
H.S.: the life and work of an American poet. *(Hilda Doolittle, 1886-1961, occasionally betrothed to Pound in Philadelphia and London, later married to Richard Aldington.)* Boston, Houghton, Mifflin, 1982. 490 p., illus. **811'.5'2.** 81-6900.

PS3531.082Z795
Rosenthal, M(acha) L(ouis)
A primer of Ezra Pound. New York, Macmillan, 1960. 56 p. Includes bibliography. *Short, brilliant study.* **811'.5'2.** 60-7281.

PS323.5/R64
Rosenthal, M.L.
Sailing into the unknown: Yeats, Pound & Eliot. New York, Oxford University Press, 1978, 224 p. Ezra Pound 77-10101.

Microfilm AC-1/no. 59-6017
Rowe, Hershel Dale, 1926-
Basic elements in the criticism of Ezra Pound. Ann Arbor, Mich., University Microfilms, 1960. Microfilm copy (positive) of typescript. Collation of the original, determined from the film: v, 253 1. Thesis— University of Florida. Abstracted in Dissertation

Abstracts, v. 20 (1960) no. 7, p. 2807-2808. Vita. Biblio.: leaves 246-252.

PS3531.082Z8/1950a & 1968
Russell, Peter, 1921-   *ed.*
An examination of Ezra Pound; a collection of essays *to be presented to Ezra Pound on his 65th birthday.* Norfolk, Conn., New Directions, 1950. *Reprinted 1968, New York: Haskell House Publishers.* 268 p. port. London ed. (P. Nevill) has title: Ezra Pound. "Select bibliography of Ezra Pound": p. 267-268. *An early landmark in the crusade to free Ezra Pound from the Washington insane asylum.* *Full name:* Irwin Peter Russell. **811.5** 50-10415.

PS3531.082P476
Ruthven, K.K.
A guide to Ezra Pound's Personae, 1926 by K.K. Ruthven. Berkeley, University of California Press, 1969.ix, 281 p. $8.50. Biblio.: p 269-281. **811'.5'2.** 69-16628. MARC.

PS3531.082Z82
San Juan, Epifanio, 1938-
Critics on Ezra Pound. Edited by E. San Juan, Jr. Coral Gables, Fla., University of Miami Press, 1972. 128 p. (Readings in literary criticism, 15.) $3.95. **811'5'2.** 70-143455. MARC. ISBN 0-87024-196-6.

PS3531.082Z833
Schneidau, Herbert N.
Ezra Pound: the image and the real. Baton Rouge, Louisiana State University Press, 1969. viii, 210 p. 5.95. Biblio. footnotes. **821'.9'12.** 75-86495. MARC. SBN 8071-0911-8.

PS3531.082Z834
Schulman, Grace
Ezra Pound: a collection of criticism. Contemporary studies in literature series. New York, McGraw-Hill, 1974. 154 p. **811'.5'2.** 74-7254.

PS3531.082Z8358
Sieburth, Richard
Instigations: Ezra Pound and Remy de Gourmont. Cambridge, Mass., Harvard University Press, 1978. 197 p. **811'.5'2.** 78-2038.

PS3531.082Z836
Simpson, Louis Aston Marantz
 Three on the tower: the lives and works of Ezra Pound, T.S.
Eliot, and William Carlos Williams. ISBN: 0688028993. 373 p.
809.1. 74-26952.

PR610.S47
Sisson, Charles Hubert, 1914-
 English poetry, 1900-1950: an assessment. London, Hart-Davis,
1971. 267 p. index. £3.50. B 71-18127. ISBN 0-246-64042-1.
821'.9'1209. 75-859486. MARC.

PS3531.082Z837
Soar, Geoffrey
 Ezra Pound in the magazines: an exhibition held in the Flazman
Gallery, 1977, London, University College London, Library, 1977.
40 p. **811'5'2.** 78-308528.

PS3531.082Z837
Soar, Geoffrey
 Ezra Pound perspectives; essays in honor of his eightieth birth-
day. Edited with an introd. by Noel Stock. Chicago, H. Regnery
Co., 1965. xii, 219 p. illus., facsims., ports. CONTENTS, Ezra
Pound: 1914, by C. Aiken, Ezra Pound, by H. Read. Tribute by M.
Moore. Leucothea's bikini: mimetic homage, by H. Kenner. Craft
and morals, by A. Alvarez. Ezra Pound and Catullus, by P.
Whigham. The search for Mrs. Wood's program, by D. Gallup.
Ezra Pound and the Bollingen prize, by A. Tate. The return of the
long poem, by H. McDiarmid. A bundle of letters. Ezra Pound and
the French language, by W. Fleming. A note on Ezra Pound, E.
Hemingway. Piers Plowman in the modern wasteland, by C.
Brooke-Rose. The Fenollosa papers. An appreciation, by T. Scott.
The rock drill, by W. Lewis. Ezra Pound, inc., by J.F. Malof. BBC
third program: Ezra Pound. Translations from the Chinese, by D.
Goacher. *An important Festschrift that also contains Ezra Pound's
autobiographical "How I Began."* **811.52.** 65-26903. Reprinted 1977,
Westport, CT,, Greenwood Press 75-40995.

PS3531.082Z838
Stock, Noel
 Ezra Pound's Pennsylvania: compiled for the most part from Mr.
Carol Gatter's researches into original sources and documents.

Toledo, Ohio, Friends of the University of Toledo Libraries, 1976. 111 p., illus. **811'.5'2.** 75-39838.

PS3531.082Z839
Stock, Noel
The life of Ezra Pound. 1st American ed. New York, Pantheon Books, 1970. London edition, Routledge & Kegan Paul, 1970. xvii, 472 p. illus., facsims, ports. 10.00 *An important biography. (See part 3)* **811'.5'2.** 73-110127. MARC.

PS3531.082Z84
Stock, Noel
Poet in exile: Ezra Pound. New York, Barnes & Noble, 1964. xi, 273 p. Biblio.: p. 261-66. **811.52.** 64-4258.

PS3531.082C288
Stock, Noel
Reading the 'Cantos': a study of meaning in Ezra Pound. London, Routledge & Kegan Paul, 1967. viii, 120 p. (B 67-3567). **811'.5'2.** 67-75833.

PS3531.082Z846
Sullivan, John Patrick   *cor.*
Ezra Pound: a critical anthology; edited by J.P. Sullivan. Harmondsworth, Penguin, 1970. 413 p. index. (Penguin critical anthologies.) (Penguin education) 12/-. B 70-28142. Biblio.: p. 379-388. *A beautifully organized model for all anthologies of everything.* ISBN 0-14-080033-6. **811'.5'2.** 73-871544. MARC.

PS3531.082H68
Sullivan, John Patrick
Ezra Pound and Sextus Propertius; a study in creative translation. Austin, University of Texas Press, 1964. x, 102 p. "Homage to Sextus Propertius, by Ezra Pound; a new text with Sexti Propertii Carmina selecta, recensuit Lucianus Mueller": p. 109-171. Biblio. footnotes. **811.52.** 64-22386.

PS3531.0820297
Surette, Leon
A light from Eleusis: a study of Ezra Pound's Cantos. Oxford, England, Clarendon Press, and New York, Oxford University Press, 1979. 306 p. **811'.5'2.** 79-311244.

PS3531.082Z85
Sutton, Walter
Ezra Pound, a collection of critical essays. Englewood Cliffs, N.J., Prentice-Hall, 1963. 184 p. (A Spectrum book: Twentieth century views. S-TC-29.) *$1.95 paperback.* Includes biblio. *and a good chronology. Contributors include W.B. Yeats, T.S. Eliot, Hugh Kenner, M.L. Rosenthal, F.R. Leavis, H.H. Watts, W.C. Williams, G.P. Elliott, W.M. Frohock, and others.* **811.52.** 63-10448.

PR737.S9
Sydney University
Some modern writers; two courses of Sydney university extension lectures, by members of the departments of English. Sydney, The Australasian medical publishing company limited, 1940. 4 p. 1., 7-119 p.
Includes Ezra Pound, by R.G. Howarth. A 42-818.

Szasz, Thomas Stephen, 1920-
Law, liberty, and psychiatry; an inquiry into the social uses of mental health practices. N. York, Macmillan, 1963. xii, 281 p. Bibl. p. 256-265. Chapter 17: "The Case of Mr. Ezra Pound." **340.6.**

PS3531.082C289
Terrell, Carroll Franklin
A companion to the Cantos of Ezra Pound. Orono, National Poetry Foundation, University of Maine, and Berkeley, University of California Press, 1978. 362 p., biblio. ISBN 0-520-03687-5. **811'.5'2 19** 78-54802.

PN1042.U2
Ueda, Makoto, 1931-
Zeami, Basho, Yeats, Pound; a study in Japanese and English poetics. The Hague, Mouton, 1965. 165 p. (Studies in general and comparative literature. v. 1.) Based on thesis, University of Washington. Biblio.: p. 157-161. **808.1.** 65-28168.

PS3531.082M4 Rare Bk. Coll.
U.S. *Library of Congress. Legislative Reference Service.*
The medical, legal, literary and political status of Ezra Weston (Loomis) Pound (1885-   ) selected facts and comments, by H.A. Sieber, research assistant, Senior Specialists Division. Rev. Apr. 14,

1958. *(It would be the time of Pound's release)*. Washington, 1958. iii, 53 p., illus.
"Prepared as a result of Congressional inquiries. Copies are not available for general distribution by the Library of Congress." Printed in the Congressional record, Daily ed., Apr. 29-30, May 6, 15, 1958. "The case of Ezra Pound" (typescript carbon copy dated May 9, 1958): 3 1. inserted. *928.1.* 58-37979.

PN1031.V54
Viereck, Peter Robert Edwin, 1916-
Dream and responsibility; four test cases of the tension between poetry and society. Washington, University Press of Washington, D.C., 1953. 65 p. **808.81.** 53-12584

PS3531.082C29
Watts, Harold Holliday, 1906-
Ezra Pound and The Cantos. Chicago, H. Regnery Co., 1952. 132 p. *The definitive book that will tell you more than you may want to know about Pound's use of pronouns and his retreat from "utter nominalism."* M.L. Rosenthal's "A primer of Ezra Pound" is briefer and better on The Cantos and reading The Cantos themselves is better still. **811.5** 53-1720.

PN4877.W45
Whittemore, Reed, 1919-
Little magazines. Minneapolis, University of Minnesota Press; distributed to high schools in the U.S. by McGraw-Hill, New York, 1963. 47 p. (University of Minnesota pamphlets on American writers, no. 32) Biblio.: p. 46-47. 63-64004.

PS3531.082Z89
Wilhelm, James J.
Dante and Pound: the epic of judgment. Orono, University of Maine Press, 1974. 187 p. 1 leaf of plates/ 74-22708.

PS3531.082C298/1977
Wilhelm, James J.
The later Cantos of Ezra Pound. New York, Walker, 1977. 221 p. illus. **811'.5'2.** 76-18472.

PS3445.I54425
Williams, William Carlos, 1883-1963.
Autobiography, New York, Random House, 1951. 402 p. 920W.

PS3545.I544Z53
Williams, William Carlos, 1883-1963.
Selected letters. Edited with an introd. by John Thirlwall. New
York: McDowell, Obolensky, 1957. 347 p. **928.1** 57-12112

PS3531.082Z9
Witemeyer, Hugh
The poetry of Ezra Pound; forms and renewal, 1908-1920.
Berkeley, University of California Press, 1969. xiv, 220 p., 6.50. In-
cludes biblio. references. **811'.5'2.** 69-13136. MARC.

PS3531.082C2897
Woodward, Anthony
Ezra Pound and The Pisan Cantos. London and Boston:
Routledge & Kegan Paul, 1980. ISBN 0-7100-0372-2. **811'.5'2.**
79-41446

PS3509.L43Z95
Wright, George Thaddeus
The poet in the poem; the personae of Eliot, Yeats, and Pound.
Berkeley, University of California Press, 1960. xii, 167 p. (Perspectives in criticism, 4.) Biblio. references included in "Notes" (p.
165-7). 808.14. 59-1448. Reissued New York, Gordian Press, 1974.
74-2404.

PL2658.E3P69
Yip, Wai-lim
Ezra Pound's Cathay. Princeton, N.J., Princeton University
Press, 1969. ix, 259 p. 7.50. "Appendix two: Cathay retranslated":
p. 181-231. Biblio.: p. 233-249. *Dedication: "for EZRA POUND if
he wants it."* 895.1'008. 68-56325. MARC.

While it has not been possible to do justice to periodicals in this
bibliography, the following are worthy of special notice:
Paideuma, "a journal devoted to Ezra Pound scholarship," is
published at Stevens Hall, University of Maine, Orono, Maine
04473.

For Pound's eighty-fifth birthday, October 30, 1970, both *Sou'wester* (literary quarterly published by Southern Illinois University at Edwardsville, $1) and *Agenda* (5 Cranbourne Court, Albert Bridge Road, London SW11, England, $2.50) published special issues in his honor. *Sou'wester* devoted its full 144 pages to Pound; *Agenda*, a sixty-page section of its 224-page issue.

D. AUDIO-VISUAL & MISCELLANY (Recordings, Films, Tapes, etc.)

Ezra Pound Reading His Poetry on two Caedmon LP records made in Washington, D.C. (1958)

Vol. 1, TC 1122: "Mouers Contemporaines," "Cantico del Sole," *Hugh Selwyn Mauberley*, and Cantos I, IV, XXXVI, and LXXXIV

Vol. 2, TC 1155: Cantos XLV, LI, LXXVI (second half) and XCIX, "The Gypsy" and "Exile's Letter."

Library of Congress ref. no. R66-1837

Ezra Pound Reads His Cantos on CMS LP Record 619 (1971): "made during the actual reading by the poet at the Spoleto Festival of Two Worlds," with jacket notes by Hugh Kenner. Cantos III, XVI, XLIX, LXXXI, XCII, CVI, and CXV.

Library of Congress ref. no. 78-752018

Ezra Pound Reading His Translations of the Confucian Odes on Spoken Arts LP record SA 1098 (1971). Produced by Olga Rudge.

Library of Congress ref. no. 75-651867

Paraphernalia: A Regalia of Madrigals from Ezra Pound: "a divertimento for soprano, tenor, baritone, trumpet, etc.," by Raymond Wilding-White, with texts by Ezra Pound from *The Classic Anthology Defined by Confucius*, on a CRI LP record 182 SD (1964).

Library of Congress ref. no. R64-587

Le Testament de Villon, an opera by Ezra Pound in Old French, with Philip Booth as Villon; Dorothy Barnhouse, John Duykers, Sandra Bush, Lawrence Cooper, and others; Western Opera Theater, Robert Hughes, conductor, on Fantasy Record 12001 (1973).

Ezra Pound: Poet's Poet ("The Literary Giant of the 20th Century

Reminisces"), a 28½ minute, 16mm. documentary "Film for the Humanities" produced by Harold Mantell (husband of one of Caedmon Records' founders). Available for purchase ($240) as film or Videocassette, or for film rental ($25) from Films for the Humanities, P.O. Box 378, Princeton, NJ 08540.

Microfilm D-19
Pound, Ezra Loomis, 1885-1972
Transcripts of shortwave broadcasts from Rome, Dec. 7, 1941-July 25, 1943. Washington, 1941-43.
Microfilm copy made in 1952 by the Library of Congress. Negative. Length of the film: 31 ft. Caption titles: Transcripts of shortwave broadcasts. Rome, issued by U.S. Federal Communications Commission. 1. World War, 1939-1945—Addresses, sermons, etc. 2. World War, 1930-1945—Italy. I. Title. Mic 52-282.

The Yale University Library has opened a Center for the Study of Erza Pound and His Contemporaries as a part of the Collection of American Literature in the Beinecke Rare Book and Manuscript Library.

The William Carlos Williams manuscript collection at Lockwood Library, State University of New York at Buffalo, has a correspondence between Pound and Williams spanning almost half a century.

In 1973, when Elliot Richardson was attorney general of the U.S., he authorized the Federal Bureau of Investigation to make its secret files on Erza Pound (and Alger Hiss, among other cases more than fifteen years old and not relevant to current investigations) public to qualified historians and scholars. As with other F.B.I. files, not all the "information" therein has been evaluated or substantiated.

5.
CHRONOLOGY: 1885 to 1972

(Grateful acknowledgment is made herewith to the tables of dates that appear in J.P. Sullivan's Penguin critical anthology and Walter Sutton's collection of critical essays, both entitled Ezra Pound. *Where dates in the Chronology do not jibe with dates in the preceding Bibliography, this is usually due to the erratic time lags between writing and publication in England, Italy, America, etc.)*

1885   Ezra Loomis Pound born on October 30, in Hailey, Idaho, to Isabel Weston Pound, a descendant of Longfellow, and Homer Loomis Pound, U.S. land recorder.

1887   Pound family goes East during Great Blizzard by train behind the first rotary snow plow. They take up residence first with Westons in New York, then a summer in Newport, then on the Pounds' ancestral farm in Wisconsin.

1889   Settles in Philadelphia, where Homer Pound has been appointed assistant assayer of ·U.S. Mint. Ezra Pound's first major exposure to money and economic talk and thought.

1898   First visit to Venice – on European tour with great-aunt.

1901-1905   Undergraduate at University of Pennsylvania (meets William Carlos Williams in 1903) and Hamilton College, Clinton, N.Y., where he receives Ph.B. degree.

1905-1906   Graduate student at University of Pennsylvania where he receives M.A. in Romance languages. Awarded a Harrison Fellowship in Romanics, he travels in Europe doing work on Spanish playwright Lope de Vega.

1907	Instructor of French and Spanish at Wabash College, Crawfordsville, Indiana, for four months. Dismissed when stranded stripper is caught sharing his room.
1908	Sails for Europe. Gibraltar, Spain, Southern France, and Venice, where his first book of poems, *A Lume Spento*, is published at his own expense, before he moves to London.
1908-1920	**RESIDENT IN LONDON**
1908	Teaches medieval Romance literature at Regent St. Polytechnic Institute.
1909	Meets W.B. Yeats and Ford Madox Ford (then Hueffer). Publishes *Personae* and *Exultations*.
1910	Meets author-painter Wyndham Lewis ("Ezra Pound is a crowd. A small crowd") and, on a brief return visit to America, patron of the arts (and, later, of T.S. Eliot) John Quinn. Publishes *Provença* and *The Spirit of Romance*, the former being first U.S. edition of his poems.
1911	Publishes *Canzoni*, dedicated to Dorothy Shakespear and her mother, Olivia.
1912	Becomes foreign correspondent of *Poetry: A Magazine of Verse*, edited in Chicago by Harriet Monroe. Publishes *The Sonnets and Ballate of Guido Cavalcanti* and *Ripostes*, in which he first defines the tenets of Imagism.
1913	*Poetry* publishes *Personae, Exultations, Canzoni,* and *Ripostes* in his native America, along with "A Few Dont's by an Imagiste." He meets Robert Frost and spends next three winters with Yeats at Stone Cottage, Sussex, acting as "Uncle William's secretary."
1914	Marries Dorothy Shakespear and brings her to live at Stone Cottage. Meets T.S. Eliot. Edits *Des Imagistes:*

An Anthology. In *Fortnightly Review,* he publishes essay on Vorticism – a literary movement (founded by Wyndham Lewis, personified by philosopher-poet T.E. Hulme, and named by Pound) that stressed abstraction, formalism, and the moving image. Contributes to and co-edits (with Wyndham Lewis) Vorticist magazine, *Blast* (1914-1915). Literary editor of *The Egoist,* in which James Joyce's *A Portrait of the Artist as a Young Man* is published.

1915   Works on Ernest Fenollosa manuscripts and publishes *Cathay.* Edits *Catholic Anthology,* including poems by Eliot. Starts work on *The Cantos.*

1916   Publishes *Lustra* and *Gaudier-Brzeska: A Memoir* of the Vorticist sculptor killed in battle. Also publishes his editing, from notes of Fenollosa, of *Noh – or Accomplishment* and *Certain Noble Plays of Japan.*

1917   First three Cantos published in *Poetry.* Becomes London editor of Margaret Anderson's *Little Review,* in which Joyce's *Ulysses* first appears in America (though book is banned in U.S. until 1933). Meets Major C.H. Douglas, the Social Credit economist, whose ideas affect Pound's monetary thinking.

1918   Publishes *Pavannes and Divagations.* Completes *Homage to Sextus Propertius.*

1919   Publishes *Quia Pauper Amavi,* which includes three Cantos and *Propertius.*

1920   Publishes *Umbra, Instigations* (including Fenollosa's essay on "The Chinese Written Character as a Medium for Poetry") and *Hugh Selwyn Mauberley.* Attends a concert by Olga Rudge, violinist, and gets to know her better. Moves to Paris.

1920-1924   **RESIDENT IN PARIS**
1920

Becomes acquainted with Gertrude Stein, Jean

Cocteau (who called Pound "a rower on the river of the dead"), Ernest Hemingway, George Antheil, and the sculptor Constantin Brancusi, among others.

1921   Publishes *Poems 1918-1921*, which includes Cantos IV-VII.

1922   Translates Remy de Gourmont's *The Natural Philosophy of Love* into English.

1923   Publishes *Indiscretions*, an "autobiographical reverie."

1924   Publishes *Antheil and the Treatise on Harmony.* Visits Italy. Begins gradual shift of base from Paris to Italy.

1925   Publishes *A Draft of XVI Cantos* . . . *July 9:* Olga Rudge gives birth to a daughter in Bressanone, Italy. Christened Maria Rudge, their daughter (later Princess Mary de Rachewiltz) is breast-fed and then taken home to live by a Tyrolean peasnt woman whose own baby has died at birth.

1926   *September 10:* Omar Shakespear Pound born in Paris to Mrs. Dorothy Shakespear Pound. . . . *Personae: The Collected Poems of Ezra Pound* is published. Pound's opera, *The Testament of François Villon* (text by Villon, *music* by Pound), premieres in concert form in Salle Pleyel, Paris.

1927-1928   Edits and publishes *The Exile,* quarterly that prints a poem by Hemingway, a chapter on E.E. Cummings from Joe Gould's *Oral History,* Yeats' *Sailing to Byzantium,* a long poem by Louis Zukofsky, and poetry and prose by William Carlos Williams, Robert McAlmon, John Cournos, and Carl Rakosi, as well as more and more of Pound's economics and attraction toward Mussolini.

1928   Settles in Rapallo.

1928-1945   RESIDENT IN ITALY

1928	Publishes *A Draft of Cantos XVII-XXVIII; Selected Poems*, with introduction by Eliot; and *Ta Hio, the Great Learning.*
1930	Publishes *A Draft of XXX Cantos* and *Imaginary Letters.*
1931	Lectures on Jefferson and Van Buren at Universitá Bocconi, Milan. Publishes *How to Read* (forerunner to *ABC of Reading*, 1934) and translation of Guido Cavalcanti, *Rime.*
1932	Edits *Profile: An Anthology.*
1933	*January 30:* Meets Mussolini. . . . Publishes *ABC of Economics*. Edits *Active Anthology.*
1934	Publishes *ABC of Reading; Eleven New Cantos: XXXI-XLI;* and *Make It New* (in Britain: U.S. edition published 1935).
1935	Publishes *Jefferson and/or Mussolini* and two pamphlets, *Social Credit: An Impact* and *Alfred Venison's Poems.*
1936	In collaboration with Olga Rudge and pianist Giorgio Levi and violinist David Nixon, initiates revival of interest in Vivaldi's music with research, concerts (in Rapallo), and articles (in Italy, England, U.S.). Fenollosa's *The Chinese Written Character* as a medium for poetry published in book form with foreword and notes by Pound.
1937	Publishes *The Fifth Decad of Cantos; Polite Essays* (in London; American edition, 1940), and *Confucius, Digest of the Analects.*
1938	Publishes *Guide to Kulchur* in England (American edition is called *Culture*).
1939	First visit to America since 1910. Receives honorary

D.Litt (Doctor of Letters) from Hamilton College. Tries to see F.D.R.; sees Henry Wallace. Publishes *What Is Money For?*. Returns to Italy, unsuccessful in Stateside mission to avert war.

1940	Begins radio broadcasting from Rome. Publishes *Cantos LII-LXXI*.
1941	Continues radio broadcasts. *December 7:* After Pearl Harbor attack, temporarily suspends broadcasting.
1942	*January 29:* Resumes broadcasts.
1943	Continues broadcasts. *July 26:* Indicted *in absentia* for treason by a U.S. grand jury in Washington. *September:* Allies land in Italy and Pound flees Rome. After visiting daughter in Tyrol, he settles in Rapallo again.
1944	In Rapallo: composes more Cantos; translates an English economics text into Italian (never published); also writes pamphlets, articles, and manifesto in Italian. Edizioni Popolari in Venice publishes Italian translations of five of Pound's works, including *Jefferson e Mussolini*.
1945	*February:* Pound's Italian version of Confucius *(The Unwobbling Pivot)* published in Venice. . . . *Spring:* arrested by Italian partisans. . . . *May 5:* Turned over to U.S. Counterintelligence in Genoa. *May 24:* Delivered to Disciplinary Training Center near Pisa and placed in solitary confinement in steel cage for three weeks. After three weeks, with health in danger, he is transferred to tent in medical compound. Writes first draft of *Pisan Cantos*. . . . *November 16:* Transferred by jeep to Rome and flown to Washington, D.C.

1945-1958   IMPRISONED IN WASHINGTON

1945	*November 18:* Remanded to District of Columbia Jail. *November 26:* New treason indictment. *December 4:*

Transferred to Gallinger Hospital in Washington for mental examination by four doctors. *December 14:* Placed in St. Elizabeth's Hospital for the Criminally Insane.

1946   *February 14:* A U.S. District Court jury pronounces him mentally unfit to stand trial and he is remanded to St. Elizabeth's indefinitely – that is, until he can stand trial for treason.

1947   *The Unwobbling Pivot and the Great Digest of Confucius* (Translation dated "D.T.C., Pisa; 5 October-5 November, 1945") published in English.

1948   *The Pisan Cantos* (LXXIV-LXXXIV) published, along with Pound's collected *Cantos.*

1949   Controversial awarding of the 1948 Bollingen Prize for Poetry to Pound for *Pisan Cantos.*

1950   *Letters of Ezra Pound, 1907-1941,* published. British poet Peter Russell starts bringing out (1950-1953) English translations of Pound's Italian *Money Pamphlets* as well as other economic and wartime writing plus a new edition of *ABC of Economics* under imprint of The Pound Press. Russell also publishes an influential collection of essays to honor Pound's sixty-fifth birthday . . . *Patria Mia,* lost in 1915, is found and published thirty-five years late.

1951   *The Confucian Analects* published.

1952   Resumes work on *The Cantos* in St. Elizabeth's.

1953   *The Translations of Ezra Pound* published.

1954   Publishes *The Classic Anthology Defined by Confucius* and *Literary Essays of Ezra Pound* (edited with introduction by Eliot).

1955   Publishes *Section Rock Drill* (Cantos LXXXV-XCV).

1956	Publishes his version of Sophocles' *Women of Trachis* in London.
1957	*Women of Trachis* published in U.S.
1958	After intervention by Frost, Hemingway, Eliot, and Archibald MacLeish, among others, treason indictment is dismissed and Pound returns to Italy to live with his daughter, Princess Mary De Rachewiltz, at her Schloss Brunnenburg, near Merano.
1958-1972	**RESIDENT IN ITALY**
1959	As relations and health deteriorate, Pound gradually moves out of Brunnenburg and begins dividing time between Rapallo and Venice. . . . Publishes *Thrones: Cantos XCVI-CIX* and completes his 111th Canto by Christmas.
1960	Publishes *Impact: Essays on the Ignorance and the Decline of American Civilization.*
1961	Treated for urinary infection in Rome hospital; recuperates in Brunnenburg; undergoes prostate surgery in Rapallo.
1962	His silences begin. The Villon-Pound opera, *Le Testament,* is broadcast by the BBC.
1964	Co-edits *Confucius to Cummings: An Anthology of Poetry.* Treated at Clinique la Prairie in Clarens, Switzerland, by Dr. Paul Niehans, noted rejuvenator and physician to Pope Pius XII, and makes substantial improvement. While in Switzerland, poses for painter Oskar Kokoschka, four months his junior.
1965	*January:* Attends funeral rites for Eliot in Westminster Abbey and visits Yeats' widow in Dublin. Canto CX is privately printed in Cambridge, Massachusetts. Chooses material for *Selected Cantos.* For Pound's eightieth birthday, Noel Stock publishes an anthology of essays in his honor, *Perspectives.*

1966	*October:* Writes brief introduction to Selected Cantos.
1967	Goes to Paris for French publication of *ABC of Reading, How to Read,* and *The Spirit of Romance.* At meeting with French critics, he maintains what is described as "obstinate silence" – but not in private meeting with Samuel Beckett. . . .*Selected Cantos* published in English. . . . Visits Joyce's grave in Switzerland.
1968	Drafts and fragments of Cantos CX-CXVII published in New York.
1969	Revisits New York briefly for first time since he sailed from there to Italy after release in 1958. Private reunions with old friends and grandson, Walter de Rachewiltz, studying at Rutgers. Attends annual meeting of Academy of American Poets in New York Public Library boardroom, but maintains silence. Also confers with Elliot's widow, Valerie, about new edition of *Waste Land.* Attends Hamilton College commencement, where his publisher, James Laughlin, receives honorary degree. Pound, in cap and gown, receives standing ovation.
1970	Collected *Cantos* (first 117 of them) published.
1971	Canto CXVIII joins the Collection. His Daughter's Book, *Discretions,* is published in Boston. Eliot's *Waste Land,* showing Pound's revision, is issued in its most complete form.
1972	*January 9:* "Ezra Pound – The Voice of Silence" appears on cover of *The New York Times Magazine.* . . . *February:* He reads in loud, clear voice at memorial service for Marianne Moore in Venice. . . . *Spring:* Emerson-Thoreau Medal for Pound vetoed in 13 to 9 vote by Governing council of American Academy of Arts and Sciences. . . . *July 4:* Pound writes foreword to *Selected Prose 1909-1965.* . . . *October 30:* Celebrates his eighty-seventh birthday. . . . *November 1, 1972:* Death in Venice.